55 AND OUT

HOW TO RETIRE WITH LIFE TO SPARE

Christopher Edwin Justice

ARRIVE FIRST, INC.

Acknowledgments

This book exists because of people, not ideas.

Lynn Scheurell gave this book its life—and without her, I would never have the words nor the motivation. Kelly Shores taught me that time is respect. Scott Howell showed me that boring works. Keith Goode, my friend of 40 years, makes certain I'm grounded. Susie Stockholm gave it honest eyes. Todd Rollin told me to trust the stories more and explain the principles less. They were all right about the things that mattered.

Andy Meadows proved that patience compounds in ways no formula can predict. Maura Thomas told me the title had to earn its shelf.

Michele married a man who asked for Iron Maiden on a dating profile and has been translating my nonsense into something livable ever since. Logan Christopher Justice, my son, reminds me every day to see the world with compassion. Adam True Justice, my other son, is my true retirement plan. My sons remind me daily why any of this matters.

My mother, Pat, taught me that joy does not wait for permission. My father, Edwin, taught me not to follow patterns of previous generations. The license plate gave me the goal without them knowing it.

I kept the promise. Close enough.

Table of Contents

Acknowledgments   *iii*

Author's Note   *ix*

How to Read This Book   *xi*

Who This Book Is For   *xiii*

Chapter 1: The Script You Didn't Write   1

A Number That Was Invented   *3*

The Map They Gave Us   *4*

The Trade   *5*

Bodies Don't Compound   *7*

The Cost of Waiting   *8*

What Wealth Actually Means   *9*

Unlearning   *11*

Chapter 2: Time Is the Asset   15

You'll Have Time   *18*

Healthspan   *18*

Useable Years   *19*

Health Sidebar   *21*

Risk and Sequence   *22*

The Old Man *24*

Scott *25*

My Ages *26*

The Modern Influence *27*

Chapter 3: The Formula **31**

Choose Your Age *35*

The Boring Formula *37*

The Gift *40*

Boredom Is a Competitive Advantage *43*

The Script of Other Societies *44*

Free Money *45*

Taxes Are Real *46*

Five Hundred Thousand *47*

Trust the System *49*

The Index Card *50*

The Foundation, Not the House *51*

The Inversion *52*

Chapter 4: Optionality Changes Everything **55**

What Optionality Actually Is *56*

Optionality Is Not Hustle *57*

What You Already Know *59*

No One Really Cares *61*

The Chain *62*

Chapter 5: The People and the Property   67

The Part That Isn't Flattering   *68*

Andy   *69*

Sticks and Stones   *71*

The Dream House   *73*

Choose Partners Like You Are Marrying Them   *74*

Chapter 6: Designing a Life Worth Living   77

What Does a Good Day Look Like?   *79*

The Enabler   *81*

The Tax That Increases   *82*

The Data   *83*

Geography Is a Financial Strategy   *85*

The Rules Are About to Change   *86*

Pay Attention to the Margins   *87*

Chapter 7: Building Your Second Life   91

Your Second Life Begins When Obligation Ends   *94*

Identity Evolves   *95*

The Comparison Trap   *96*

Stuff   *97*

Money Is Not the Enemy   *98*

Optional Work   *99*

Chapter 8: Arrival　　**103**

Others Notice　　*104*

The Need to Explain Fades　　*105*

What This Book Was Really About　　*106*

The Index Card　　*107*

Do This Now　　*108*

Not Arriving Late　　*110*

The Dividend　　*110*

You Are Already Enough　　*112*

My Parents' Son　　*112*

About the Author　　*115*

Author's Note

My parents had this license plate that you see on the cover.

It hung on the back of their car for years, a declaration, a goal, a promise to themselves. They were going to retire at fifty-five. They were going to do what most people only talk about. They put it on the car so they couldn't forget.

They never made it.

My father retired at sixty-seven, his body worn out. My mother took an early pension at sixty, smiled through the uncertainty, and remained generous with money she didn't have.

I have this license plate now. It sits in my office, visible on every Zoom call. A reminder of what they wanted. A reminder of what didn't happen. A reminder that wanting something and building something are not the same.

This book is for my mother.

Not because she asked for it. She would tell me to stop making a fuss. But because she taught me something I had to unlearn and then relearn: that joy does not wait for permission, that wealth is not the same as money, and that a life can be full regardless of what the account says.

She lived with poverty and she lived with plenty. Her essential nature never changed between the two. That consistency puzzled me for years. Now I understand it. She knew what actually mattered. I had to spend decades figuring out what she already knew.

This book exists because the script my parents followed was broken, and they knew it was broken. That is why they put that plate on their car. They could see what they wanted, even if they couldn't escape it in time.

I did. At fifty-four, I walked away. Kind of.

55 and Out is the book they couldn't write, built from the life they helped me see. It is a case for building freedom early, so life is lived forward, not deferred.

Each of us has the opportunity to live twice. Two different lives. The first driven by ambition and the pursuit of money. The second by purpose and joy.

You do not need to wait. You do not need permission.

Decide. 55 and Out.

How to Read
This Book

This book is not a financial plan. It is not a step-by-step retirement guide. It will not tell you how much to save each month or which index fund to buy. There are better books for that, and I will point you to some of them.

What this book will do is change how you think about time, money, and freedom. Not your money: your time. Not your portfolio: your life.

The first half of this book is reflective. It asks you to examine the assumptions you have been carrying, many of them inherited, most of them unexamined, about when life is supposed to begin. The second half gets more practical. It gives you frameworks, tools, and hard-won lessons for building a life you do not need to retire from.

Not prescriptive. I'm not your financial advisor, and I don't play one on podcasts. However, there will be examples tangible enough that you can do something with them if you're ready. Things I ignored for years, then finally applied, only to discover they had been true all along.

You can read it straight through. You can skip to the chapters that feel most urgent. You can read it once, put it down, and come back to it in five years when the words hit differently. That is how the best books work. They wait for you.

Who This Book Is For

You did everything right. Got the degree, got the job, climbed the ladder, paid the bills. And somewhere around year twenty, you looked up and thought: wait, this is it?

You are not lazy. You are not ungrateful. You are starting to realize that the system you bought into was designed to keep you productive, not fulfilled. And you are wondering whether there is another way.

This book is for the person who has done well enough to feel guilty about wanting more. Who has money in the bank but feels poor in time. Who looks at their calendar and sees obligations where there used to be possibilities.

It is for the person in their thirties wondering if it's too early to think about this. It is for the person in their fifties wondering if it's too late. It is for the spouse who keeps hearing "someday" and wants to know when someday arrives.

If someone handed it to you, they're trying to tell you something. Let them.

This is not a book about being rich. It is a book about being free. Freedom, in this context, means one thing: the ability to decide how you spend your day. That is the definition of wealth this book operates on. Everything else is accounting.

I'm not writing from a mountain. I'm writing from the other side of a mess I eventually figured out. I lost three fortunes by age forty. I co-signed businesses that failed. I watched my own parents struggle with a retirement system that was never designed to work for them. And I still made it to the other side.

One more thing. This book is for my kids and their kids.

If it helps you too, that is the best outcome I can imagine.

CHAPTER 1

The Script You Didn't Write

*"The trouble with the rat race is that
even if you win, you're still a rat."*
— Lily Tomlin

* * *

"I don't know what I'm supposed to do now," he said.

My father retired at sixty-seven. Not because he planned to. Not because he wanted to. His body simply refused to do the work that he had done before. Forty-one years in pest control, and his body was worn. I helped him start his final company. I co-signed it and helped him sell it so he could retire. But he couldn't stop. He worked for the new owner and kept finding new side jobs. Every time I asked why, he had the same answer.

My mother retired earlier at sixty. She took an early pension and lived carefree. She smiled and was always too generous with her money.

They had followed the script perfectly. Work hard. Stay loyal. Save what you can. Retire when you're told it's time. The script promised that the ending would feel like relief, like reward. Instead, it felt like waking up in a foreign country without a map. They divorced in their sixties, splitting a small nest egg and living off Social Security.

I'm not sure my father will find what he is looking for. The travel he had postponed will never happen. Ecuador was a plan. It stayed a plan. The energy for it had been spent decades earlier. The freedom he had earned arrived in a body that could no longer fully use it.

I think about my dad often. Not with blame, not with pity. With understanding. He did what he was taught to do. He followed the only script he was given. The problem was never my father.

My mother grew up equally poor. When her job produced income, she spent it. When my parents started a business together, they spent that too. My mother lived well and was overly generous. Investing was never something my parents ever really believed in. Retirement was too far away to be of concern. Kids, cars, houses, food, vacations, and stuff. My parents followed a script designed by previous generations.

I followed equally in their footsteps. The same patterns and the same script until I saw another example. My parents were not the problem.

The problem was the script itself.

* * *

A Number That Was Invented

There is a story most of us inherit before we are old enough to question it. The story goes something like this: You grow up. You go to school. You get a job. You work for forty or forty-five years. Somewhere in your sixties, you stop working. Then you rest.

This story is so deeply embedded in our culture that it feels less like a story and more like a law of nature. Gravity pulls things down. Water flows to the sea. People work until they're sixty-five.

But the number sixty-five is not a law of nature. It is not written into our biology. It is not the inevitable result of how humans are meant to live. It is, quite simply, a number that was invented, and invented recently in the long sweep of human history.

In 1881, Otto von Bismarck, the Chancellor of Germany, proposed the world's first government-run retirement system. The original retirement age was set at seventy. At that time, life expectancy in Germany was roughly forty-five years.

The pension kicked in at seventy. Most people died at forty-five.

This was not a retirement plan. It was a system designed with the quiet confidence that most workers would be gone long before they could collect. The pension was never meant to fund decades of leisure. It was meant to keep the rare survivor from dying in the streets. A safety net with holes large enough to let most people fall through on schedule.

When the United States created Social Security in 1935, the retirement age was set at sixty-five. Life expectancy at the time was around sixty-one. The German system had been reduced to the same age in 1916. Same math, different continent. The system was designed with the assumption that most people would never collect it, or would collect it for only a few years.

The script we inherited, work until sixty-five then enjoy your golden years, was never designed for the world we live in now. It was designed for a world where most people did not reach sixty-five. It was designed for a world where work was primarily physical and bodies wore out in predictable ways. It was designed for a world where corporations offered pensions and a single income could support a family and buy a home.

That world is gone. The script remains.

* * *

The Map They Gave Us

Understanding where the script came from does not mean blaming anyone for following it. The parents who taught us to aim for sixty-five were not lying to us. They were passing on the best map they had.

Context matters. A parent who entered the workforce in 1975 or 1985 lived in a different economic reality. Pensions still existed. Company loyalty was often rewarded with job security. Housing costs, adjusted for inflation, were a fraction of what they are today. A single income really could provide a stable middle-class life for a family of four.

Under those conditions, the script made sense. Work hard, stay put, trust the system.

The advice was not wrong for its time. It was simply time-bound. Every generation inherits beliefs from the generation before. Some of those beliefs are timeless. Some are deeply contextual. The challenge is telling the difference. The belief that hard work matters is probably timeless. The belief that you should stay at one company for forty years is not. The belief that saving money is wise is timeless. The belief that sixty-five is the right age to stop working is not.

What our parents gave us was their context, not their errors. They told us what they knew. Many of them are only now, in their sixties and seventies, discovering that the script did not deliver what it promised. They are not failures. They are evidence that the script itself was flawed.

*　*　*

The Trade

The most dangerous part of the script is not the number sixty-five. It is the assumption hidden beneath the number: that time moves at a constant speed, and that the years you defer today can be fully reclaimed tomorrow.

This assumption is wrong.

When you are eight years old, a year is one-eighth of your entire life. It feels enormous. Summer seems to last forever. When you are forty, a year is one-fortieth of your life. It feels shorter. Summers blur together. Entire years begin to slip past without memorable distinction.

This is not just psychology. It is mathematics. Each year you live becomes a smaller fraction of your total experience. The subjective experience of time compresses as you age. The decade between fifty-five and sixty-five will feel shorter than the decade between twenty-five and thirty-five. Not because clocks run faster, but because you do.

The script asks you to trade your longest years, the years that feel most expansive, when time moves most slowly, for the promise of freedom in your shortest years. It asks you to defer living until the years when life accelerates past you. This is not a wise trade. It is a trick of accounting, made to sound reasonable by a culture that treats time as infinitely fungible.

Time is not fungible. A year at thirty is not equivalent to a year at sixty. The experiences available to you, the energy you bring to those experiences, the physical capacity to engage with the world, all of these change with age. Not always for the worse, but always changing. The freedom to hike a mountain at thirty is not the same as the freedom to hike a mountain at seventy. Both may be valuable. They are not interchangeable.

At the time of this writing, I am fifty-four, semi-retired, and I feel like I must capture the essence of every day. Smile more. Live with joy. Sleep as much as possible and not worry about money. I am fit enough to climb the mountain but not strong enough to survive the fall from it. Fifty to seventy are the best years of your life. This is where to really live, spend, and make the most memories possible.

Every year after seventy is a gift and should be filled with laughter and stories.

To hammer this point further, look at the comedians who lived past eighty-five: Dick Van Dyke, Bob Hope, George Burns, Betty White, Mel Brooks, Carl Reiner, Don Rickles, Phyllis Diller, Jerry Lewis, Milton Berle, Sid Caesar, and Norm Crosby.

What they shared wasn't just genetics or luck. It was life-long engagement, telling stories, laughter, and joy. They kept creating, connecting, and finding humor in the world long after traditional retirement age said they should slow down.

So be funny and happy.

* * *

Bodies Don't Compound

There is a parallel truth that the script ignores entirely: bodies do not compound.

We are taught, correctly, that money compounds. A dollar invested at twenty-five can become many dollars by sixty-five, given time and patience and the mathematics of growth. This is true and important and worth understanding.

But the logic of compounding applies to money precisely because money has no physical form. Money does not age. It does not get tired. It does not develop arthritis or heart disease or the slow erosion of energy that comes with every passing decade.

Money disappears quickly and we give it little thought. However, as we age, our friends and family begin to disappear more quickly and each loss compounds. We send fewer messages and attend more funerals.

Bodies do the opposite of compounding. Bodies depreciate. Not in a dramatic, sudden way most of the time, but in the slow accumulation of limits. The knee that aches when you climb stairs. The back that protests after a long flight. The energy that flags by mid-afternoon when it once carried you through until midnight.

This depreciation is not failure. It is biology.

The script encourages us to believe that we can compound our money for forty years and then spend it freely, as if the body that earned the money will be waiting unchanged to enjoy it. This is magical thinking.

None of us know, at twenty-five or thirty-five, which body we will have at sixty-five. The script asks us to bet everything on being the exception. That is a dangerous bet. Money you fail to accumulate can, in theory, be earned later. Years spent waiting cannot be recovered. Health that deteriorates does not return to baseline because your retirement account finally crossed a certain number.

* * *

The Cost of Waiting

The costs of waiting are not just physical. They are also psychological and emotional. There is a quieter erosion that happens when decades pass in a mode of deferral, when the answer to "What do you want to do with your life?" is always "Someday, when I can afford to."

The person who waits until sixty-five to begin living the life they actually want has spent forty years practicing a different skill: the skill of putting off. The skill of telling themselves that fulfillment is always somewhere in the future, never available in the present.

This becomes a habit. And habits, built over decades, do not disappear the moment a retirement account reaches a target number. The person who has practiced deferral for forty years often finds that deferral has become their default mode. They finally have the time and the money, but they no longer remember what they wanted to do with either. Or they remember, but they no longer trust themselves to pursue it.

This is what my father found in his garage, surrounded by old cars he would never restore. The freedom had arrived, but the capacity to use it had been gradually worn away by decades of postponement, divorce, and health issues. He had practiced waiting so long that he no longer knew how to stop.

* * *

What Wealth Actually Means

The word "wealth" is part of what needs unlearning. We use the word as if it means one thing, when it actually means several different things that are often in tension with each other.

In common usage, wealth means money. Net worth. The number at the bottom of a financial statement. This is the simplest definition, and it is useful for certain purposes, but it is also dangerously incomplete.

There is another definition of wealth that matters more for the questions this book is asking. Wealth, in this second sense, means the freedom to choose how you spend your days. Not someday, not after you reach a certain number, but now, in your current life. A person who has this freedom is wealthy in the deepest sense, regardless of their net worth. A person who lacks this freedom is not truly wealthy, no matter how large their accounts.

Money can buy freedom, but it does not automatically do so. Plenty of people with high net worth live lives of quiet constraint, trading their time for more money they do not need, because they never learned to translate money into freedom. And plenty of people with modest net worth live lives of remarkable freedom, because they understood early that freedom was the point, and they built their lives accordingly.

When we talk about retiring at fifty-five instead of sixty-five, we are not primarily talking about accumulating more money faster. We are talking about understanding what money is for. Money is a tool. The purpose of the tool is to build a life of freedom. The moment you forget this, the moment money becomes the goal rather than the means, you have lost the plot.

Freedom of choice means having the ability to decide, on any given day, how you will spend that day. Most of us begin our working lives without this freedom. We take jobs that dictate where we must be, when we must be there, and what we must do while we are there. This is normal. This is how young people without capital trade their time for money. It is not shameful. It is starting.

The question is not whether you start without freedom. Nearly everyone does.

The question is whether you treat that condition as permanent or temporary. The person who treats it as permanent makes decisions that lock in their dependence: the expensive apartment, the car payment, the lifestyle that requires every paycheck. The person who treats it as temporary makes different decisions: the smaller apartment, the paid-off car, the lifestyle that leaves room to breathe. Both people earn the same salary. One is building toward freedom. The other is building a more elaborate prison.

* * *

Unlearning

If the old script is broken, what replaces it?

The first step is not a new plan. The first step is unlearning. Unlearning the assumptions that were handed to us. Unlearning the belief that sixty-five is a magical number. Unlearning the idea that freedom is something you earn at the end of your working life, rather than something you can build into your life from the beginning.

Unlearning is harder than learning. When you learn something new, you add to what you already know. When you unlearn, you have to let go of something that felt true. You have to admit that a belief you organized your life around may not serve you. This is uncomfortable. It can feel like betrayal.

But unlearning is not betrayal. It is updating. It is recognizing that the map you were given was drawn for a different territory. The territory has changed. The map must change too.

The specific beliefs that need unlearning will vary from person to person. But there are common threads. The belief that work must consume the best hours of your best years. The belief that freedom is earned only through decades of sacrifice. The belief that wanting more from life before sixty-five is naive or greedy or unrealistic.

These beliefs were not invented to harm you. They emerged from specific historical conditions and were passed down because they once worked, or at least seemed to. But their time has passed. Holding onto them now is not loyalty. It is limitation.

To the parents reading this: none of what I am describing is meant as criticism of your choices or your generation. The world you navigated was different. The options available to you were different. You raised children, paid mortgages, handled crises, and built whatever stability you could with the tools you were given. That is not nothing. That is everything.

This book is for you, all parents. These words are the invitation for you to tell your story to your kids and grandkids. Each generation influences.

The greatest gift we can give our children is permission. Permission to question the script. Permission to want more than forty years of work followed by tired freedom. Permission to build lives that do not defer meaning until it is too late to enjoy it.

To the young adults reading this: the script you inherited was not designed to serve you. It was designed to serve a different economy, a different life expectancy, a different world. The people who handed it to you were not trying to mislead you. They were passing on what they knew.

But you are not obligated to follow a script simply because it was handed to you. You are allowed to ask whether the script still makes sense. You are allowed to notice that the path to sixty-five feels endless and the reward at the end feels uncertain. You are allowed to want something different.

Wanting something different is not laziness. It is not entitlement. It is the recognition that your life is finite, that your time is non-renewable, that the years ahead of you, however many there are, are yours to shape.

Today, you have more power than you think. Not because the world is easy. It is not. But because you are early. You have years ahead to make different choices. Every year you start sooner is a year of freedom gained on the back end. Every assumption you question now is a constraint you do not carry forward.

I return to my father in the garage, surrounded by tools he will never use and cars he will never restore.

He was not a failure. He was a man who followed the only script he knew. The script failed him, not the other way around. He worked hard and stayed loyal and saved what he could, and in the end, the reward was a body too tired to enjoy what he had earned and a mind that had forgotten how to live without the structure of work.

The script he followed was not his fault. But you have something he did not: the chance to see the script for what it is. A story, not a law. A historical accident, not an inevitability. A map drawn for a territory that no longer exists.

The next question is simpler and harder: if the script was wrong about when to stop, what else was it wrong about? Start with time. That is the asset no script can give you back.

*   *   *

Questions Worth Sitting With

1. When you wake up tomorrow, will it feel like a day you chose or a day that was assigned to you? Where is the line between the two?

2. What is the first belief about work, retirement, or money that you inherited from your parents? Do you still carry it? Does it still fit?

3. If joy were the metric instead of income, how would you measure whether your life is working?

4. Are you investing in your future self, or are you investing in a future version of your life that may never arrive?

5. What would it take for you to wake up and feel like every day is a vacation, not from responsibility, but from obligation?

CHAPTER 2

Time Is the Asset

"The trouble is, you think you have time."
—Jack Kornfield

* * *

I started my second company in 2007 after I successfully failed on a few other endeavors. I joined a group of so-called entrepreneurs and learned some new skills. One of the most important skills I learned was that you can't do it alone, so you find people with intelligence and you convince them to join up with you.

In my days in the tech sector, I met a guy named T. Kelly Shores. I won't tell you his first name because he prefers Kelly and that's a sign of respect. He was brilliant, charming, and an incredible marketing professional. Video, branding, graphic design, he knew it all, so after some time, we built an agency together. I learned so much from him.

In the early days, I was always late but I had good excuses.

Kelly was a man of time. He worked on production teams, large conferences with tens of thousands of people. If the show starts at 8 AM, you're there at 5 AM, you rehearse and you start exactly at 8 . . . on the dot.

One day, I was late for a meeting, an important meeting with Target. Big company, with our small agency in a tiny office. We didn't even have enough proper seating. What we had was a collection of massive sofa seats. Kelly dragged them all into the conference room. When the Target executives arrived—women in business suits and short skirts—they had to lower themselves into these deep, oversized cushions until they were practically sitting on the floor. We stood above them and presented our plan. It was absurd. It was confident.

I was late.

Kelly came to me after the meeting and said something that changed my life forever.

"When we choose a time and you are late, it's like you're spitting in my face. It is the ultimate form of disrespect," he said.

That echoed in my head. I replayed that in my head for weeks and recalled a lifetime of late arrivals, missed flights, penalties, and punishments for not being on time.

I wanted to argue. I wanted to explain that I was busy, that I had been pulled in too many directions, that the meeting with Target was important, but not the only thing on my plate. But I could not argue with truth. Kelly was right. Every late arrival was a declaration: my time matters more than yours. I had been making that declaration my entire adult life without hearing it.

From that day forward, I was the first at the office. I showed respect for another person's time so much that I was often an hour early for every meeting. I now go to the airport four to six hours before my flight.

I know. Michele says I didn't cure the disease, I just caught a different one. Michele is my wife. She is Brazilian, from São Paulo, and when you are married to someone who translates your words and actions through a second language and a different culture, you learn quickly that what you mean and what lands are not always the same thing. She has a way of seeing through my justifications that no American English speaker has ever managed. She's not wrong.

I used to crap on other people's time. Now I shit on my own. I sit in airport lounges for five hours, watching CNBC on mute, eating free nuts like a nervous squirrel. At least this version comes with unlimited drinks and you can never have enough Tumi luggage.

Small events can have a profound impact on your life and your respect of time.

This chapter is about your time. Not time management, not productivity hacks, not squeezing more output from your hours. What matters here is the recognition that time is the non-renewable asset. Everything else you might accumulate—money, possessions, even relationships—can in theory be rebuilt if lost. Time cannot. The hour you spent today is gone. The year you are living now will not return.

Wasting time, or worse, the lack of recognition of your time, is the single greatest mistake a human can make.

* * *

You'll Have Time

In 2004, William Shatner and Ben Folds collaborated on a spoken-word piece called "You'll Have Time" that states this truth with uncomfortable directness. Over Folds' piano arrangement, Shatner lists the dead: his parents, presidents, Johnny Cash, Einstein, Joey Ramone—and repeats the obvious fact we spend our lives avoiding. You are going to die. You can't predict the date but you can plan for it.

The song is absurd and sincere in equal measure, almost comedic in its bluntness, yet it lands because it says what polite conversation refuses to say. The refrain circles back to regret: the dying person who suddenly has time to wonder why they wasted it, why they did not taste it. The song offers no comfort, no afterlife, no redemption, only the observation that this knowledge is available now, before the end, while there is still time to act on it. Most of us hear the message and nod, then return to living as if it does not apply to us.

I met Mr. Shatner in 2012 and thanked him for his work. He's still alive and working at the time of this writing. I listen to the song every time I need motivation. He invested and spent his time well.

∗ ∗ ∗

Healthspan

There is a difference between lifespan and healthspan. Lifespan is how long you live. Healthspan is how long you live in a condition that allows you to do the things you want to do.

In developed countries, average lifespan now stretches into the late seventies or early eighties. This is a remarkable achievement of modern medicine, sanitation, and safety. A child born today has a reasonable chance of seeing ninety.

But healthspan has not kept pace with lifespan. The average person spends the final years of life in diminished capacity. Not necessarily bedridden, but constrained. Mobility limits what they can do. Energy limits how much they can do. Chronic conditions require management and accommodation. The years are there, but the years are not the same.

What's the point in saving or retiring at seventy if you are bedridden.

The gap between lifespan and healthspan is where the script fails most completely. The script promises that you can work until sixty-five and then enjoy your remaining years. But if healthspan effectively ends at seventy or seventy-five for many people, the script is offering five to ten years of compromised freedom as the reward for forty years of labor. The math does not favor the worker.

This is not pessimism. It is demography. Some people maintain robust health into their eighties and beyond. These people exist, and their existence is wonderful. But they are not the median outcome. Planning your life around being exceptional is not a plan. It is a hope dressed up as a strategy. History has proven that gambling has more losers than winners.

* * *

Useable Years

The concept of useable years clarifies what is actually at stake. Useable years are the years in which you have the health, energy, and motivation to do the things that matter to you. For most people, useable years are concentrated earlier in life than the script suggests.

The Prime: twenty-five to forty. Your body is at or near peak capacity. Recovery is fast. Energy is high. You can travel rough, sleep on floors, eat badly, and bounce back. These are the years of maximum physical optionality. They are also the years the script tells you to spend entirely on career building. The trade is invisible while you are making it.

The Pivot: forty to fifty-five. The body is still strong but the signals of decline have arrived. Recovery takes longer. Injuries linger. Sleep matters more. You cannot do everything you could at thirty, but you can still do most of it. This is the window where the smartest people begin restructuring. Not because they are failing but because they can see the curve. The ones who wait until the curve hits them have fewer options.

The Selection: fifty-five to seventy. You can still skydive at sixty-three. I jumped from a plane at thirty-five and today, at almost fifty-five, I have no desire to do that again. You can still travel, hike, surf, build. But you are selecting from a narrower menu. The body that once said yes to everything now says yes to some things and not yet to others and never again to a few. The person who arrives here without having used The Prime and The Pivot has a smaller set of experiences available than the person who spent those years deliberately.

After seventy, the menu narrows further. This is not pessimism. It is biology. And the retirement script asks you to start ordering from the menu only after the best items have been removed.

* * *

Health Sidebar

In the Netflix series *Live to 100: Secrets of the Blue Zones*, author Dan Buettner travels to places like Okinawa, Japan, and other Blue Zones where people regularly live into their nineties and hundreds. What stands out isn't biohacking or supplements. It's mundane, almost boring: daily movement, strong social ties, simple food, and bodies that are still being used. These people don't "exercise" so much as they never stop moving in natural ways. Gardening, walking, carrying, standing, sitting, and standing again.

One detail shows up repeatedly if you watch closely: they can squat. Not gym squats. Life squats. Full down, heels on the ground, and back up again without drama. Squatting requires hip flexibility, balance, leg strength, and coordination, all things that quietly disappear when chairs replace floors and convenience replaces movement. The ability to squat and stand is one of the simplest predictors of long-term mobility. Lose it, and balance goes next. Then walking changes. Then falls happen. This isn't about fitness. It's about not becoming fragile while you're still alive.

And then there's the least glamorous topic of all: toilets. Modern sitting toilets may be comfortable, but they've removed one of the last daily movements that kept hips flexible and core muscles engaged. For most of human history, bowel movements required a squat. Now we sit, we strain, and we wonder why our hips are tight, our balance is off, and our backs hurt. It's funny until it isn't. Longevity isn't just about living longer. It's about being able to get down, get up, walk steadily, and yes, go to the bathroom without assistance.

Civilization solved many problems. It quietly created a few new ones too.

Flexibility is one secret to a long life. Squat and squat often.

* * *

Risk and Sequence

If time is the asset and useable years are concentrated earlier in life, why does the script have us spending those years almost entirely on work and accumulation?

The answer is compounding. Compounding is the most powerful force in finance. A dollar invested early grows to many dollars over time because the returns themselves generate returns. A person who invests consistently from age twenty-five to sixty-five will accumulate far more than a person who invests twice as much from age forty-five to sixty-five. Time in the market matters more than timing the market. Early money is worth more than late money because it has more time to grow.

This is true, and it is important. But the script contains a hidden assumption: that maximizing wealth is the goal. And this assumption deserves scrutiny.

The key insight is that compounding needs decades, not intensity. A person who saves a moderate amount for thirty-five years will typically outperform a person who saves an aggressive amount for fifteen years, simply because the first person gave the money more time to grow.

If the last ten years of work contribute relatively little to your ultimate wealth compared to the first ten years, then why are we spending them as if they were essential? The answer, I suspect, is that the script was not designed to optimize your life. It was designed to optimize something else: employer access to experienced workers, government pension funding, the inertia of established systems. The script is not evil, but it is not yours.

I had lost three fortunes by the time I was forty. I moved on and built something new because I was young. In fact, I kept hustling just to hustle. Easy Communities, Justice Pest Services, King Florist, Justice Strategy, Leading Reach, Sparksight, High Attendance, EyeFrame, HackTech, BL.INK, Captix, and the list went on.

Risk tolerance changes with age. When you are young, risk is tolerable because you have time to recover from failure. A business that fails at thirty is a learning experience. At fifty-five, it might be a catastrophe. The young are wired for risk in ways the old are not. This is biology, not character.

The script ignores this window. It assumes you can work until sixty-five, accumulate your resources, and then suddenly transform into a person who takes bold action with their freedom. But that is not how humans work. The person who has spent forty years avoiding risk does not become a risk-taker overnight. The habits of caution, the preference for security, the diminished appetite for novelty, these are not switched off by the arrival of a pension.

If you want to take risks, to start something, to try something, to live in a way that requires courage, the time to do it is when you have both the capacity for recovery and the psychological appetite for risk. Waiting until sixty-five means waiting until both have faded.

*   *   *

The Old Man

My father is seventy-five. He works at a nudist resort in Florida. I will let that sit for a moment.

He moved to Florida to be near me. That was the plan, anyway. Proximity was supposed to help. It did not. He got divorced late in life, split a small nest egg, and lives on Social Security. He is frugal. He keeps busy. He works home improvement jobs, does substitute teaching, and yes, provides security at a nudist resort, which is exactly the kind of Florida detail that sounds like a joke. It is a joke. He would want you to laugh.

But underneath the joke is something harder. My father's body reflects the decisions of a very difficult childhood and a lifetime of physical work. His knees, his back, his hands. They carry the record of every job he ever took, every load he ever lifted, every year he traded for a paycheck. Moving to Florida did not make him happy. Nothing seems to anymore. He is not miserable. He is just searching. He has been searching since he retired at sixty-seven, and he has not found what he is looking for.

The thing I keep coming back to is that he was happier in his fifties. When the work was hard but the body could still do it. When the days had structure that he chose rather than structure that was imposed. When the future still felt like something he could shape. Somewhere between fifty-five and sixty-seven, the window closed. Not all at once. Slowly, the way a door shuts when no one is pushing it.

I want you to feel this. Not as sympathy for my father. He does not need your sympathy. Feel it as a warning. The regret of a life not lived is quieter than you expect. It does not arrive as a crisis. It arrives as a Tuesday afternoon when you realize you cannot remember the last time you did something that mattered to you. And then another Tuesday. And then a year of Tuesdays.

However, at any age, working gives you purpose and flow. When you're young you'll be inspired by everything and everyone. As you grow and begin to see the world differently, you'll start to form a date or age that feels good to you. The day that you'll say goodbye, when you'll move from ambition to purpose.

I wanted to be rich. My freedom came after the wanting had gone.

* * *

Scott

My friend Scott Howell graduated the same year I did, from the same high school. He went to work at Lowe's. Not corporate. Not an executive. Just steady, dependable work. He has a thick Southern accent, the kind that makes people underestimate him within the first five seconds. He's a simple man in the best sense of the word. Methodical, patient, and quietly disciplined.

He followed me into computer science at the University of North Carolina. On paper, our paths looked similar, but the outcomes couldn't have been more different. I chased opportunity, titles, and higher salaries. Scott chased consistency. He saved early. He invested simply. He avoided lifestyle creep. He never tried to look successful.

Scott retired at forty-two. A millionaire. No headlines. No victory lap.

What still stops me cold is this: Scott earned substantially less than I did over his career, yet he retired fifteen years before me. Not because he was smarter, luckier, or more ambitious, but because he decided early what "enough" looked like and never moved the goalposts.

Scott didn't retire from work. He retired from obligation. And he did it quietly, while the rest of us were still telling ourselves we'd get serious "later."

* * *

My Ages

I do not know how many useable years I have left. No one does. But I know the number is finite, and I know it is smaller than it was ten years ago, and I know it will be smaller still ten years from now. Had I taken the time to study time, I would have realized the simplicity and purpose of life is simply joy. So I defined my joy.

At fifty-five, I stop working hard. Not stop working. Stop working hard. The difference matters.

At sixty, I travel full time. Not vacations. Full time. Every month a different place.

At sixty-five, I settle somewhere warm and keep moving, but slower.

At seventy, I find a small village with a simple rhythm and I stay.

Everything beyond that is a gift.

Therefore, whatever I have invested, I will spend the most between fifty-five and seventy. Fifteen years of tasting the world before telling stories to strangers.

You do not need my numbers. You need your own. But you need them now, while the menu is still full.

* * *

My mother and father started learning about money and decided to anchor their lives into retiring at fifty-five. They were so passionately devoted to this endeavor they put a license plate on their car. I have it in my office to this day, thirty years later. It appears in every Zoom call I do.

My parents never achieved the ambitious title of this book.

Maybe they were never meant to.

Some people live simply to inspire others.

Time is the asset you cannot earn back. Spend it with that understanding, and many other decisions become clearer.

* * *

The Modern Influence

My son came home from school after his economics class and asked to talk. He explained to me that he didn't want to go to college. He was worried about student loan debt. He provided examples of doctors and lawyers who after twenty years of work still had debt.

"Of all debts out there, student loans are the worst and I don't want that," he said.

So now, instead of the benefit of education, the fear of debt is resulting in a denial of the benefits of education. Whereas his generation fears debt, our generation embraced it in the trillions.

I asked him to consider the alternative. College doesn't teach skills. It teaches relationship building. This is why Harvard and other Ivy League schools grow successful businesses. Entrepreneurs and funding are not born out of skills or innovation but out of long-lived relationships. The same kind of relationship I had with Andy Meadows, a connection made in 2006 that changed my financial life twenty years later. That did not come from a classroom. It came from showing up, being curious, and staying in touch. But it started because two people were in the same room at the same time.

College is one room. Work is another. A conference is another. The room matters less than what you do once you're in it. But you have to be in a room.

* * *

You've made it this far. You've done the hardest part already. Not the math. Not the accounts. Not the mechanics. You heard a message. You've questioned the script. You've acknowledged time. That alone puts you ahead of where most people ever arrive.

Up to this point, everything has been about clearing the ground, removing inherited beliefs, redefining what "wealth" actually means, and deciding that your life deserves intention, not delay. Without that foundation, formulas don't work. They're ignored, abandoned, or misused.

Now the pattern is clear: Wealth is freedom. Time gives wealth.

In the next chapter, we move from philosophy to practice. This is where patience becomes a strategy, boredom becomes an advantage, and the future starts working for you instead of against you.

* * *

Questions Worth Sitting With

1. If you measured your life by time remaining rather than money accumulated, what would you do differently this week?

2. Who is the first person you know who stopped working before forty? What did they know that you didn't? If you don't know anyone, what does that tell you about the circles you move in?

3. Which band are you in right now: The Prime, The Pivot, or The Selection? What experiences are available to you today that will not be available in ten years?

4. Can you see yourself building a life that doesn't require you to be obligated to a job? What would the first morning of that life feel like?

5. Has anyone ever said something to you, one sentence, that permanently changed how you behave? What was it?

CHAPTER 3

The Formula

*"The stock market is a device for transferring
money from the impatient to the patient."*
—Warren Buffett

* * *

My mom talks to everyone.

She's seventy-four and she does it without effort or intention. The woman next to her in line. The cashier. The person sitting alone. She doesn't dominate conversations or perform warmth. She simply opens the door. A comment. A question. A shared observation. That's it. This behavior drives my father and sister absolutely mad.

My father is seventy-five and the opposite. He lives alone. He talks to almost no one. No small talk. No curiosity about strangers. No loose threads of connection. Same era. Two radically different social realities.

I've spent years thinking about health, longevity, systems, and optimization. What I've come to understand is simpler than anything sold to us: the more you talk real talk, human talk, the longer and better you tend to live. Not because conversation is magic, but because isolation is corrosive.

You don't need to "learn the language" of connection. You already know the vocabulary. Hello. How are you. That's interesting. Tell me more. Most people aren't waiting for brilliance. They're waiting for permission to exist out loud. Pick a stranger. Say good day or I like your coat.

My mother doesn't network. She doesn't build communities on purpose. She just starts where things are easiest. She speaks. Then listens. Then repeats. Over time, layers of meaning, trust, and belonging form. Not engineered. Accumulated.

We overcomplicate wellness. We reach for intelligence before we master the obvious. Talk to people first. Add sophistication later, if needed. Health doesn't begin in isolation or optimization. It begins in contact. That's the origin of this book. Someone told me to do it.

So now, this chapter is a reminder: you are always talking to someone, including yourself. Choose the simplest words. Use them often.

I begin with my mother because building wealth works the same way.

*   *   *

My friend Scott Howell graduated the same year I did, from the same high school. He went to work at Lowe's. He stayed at Lowe's. For twenty years, he showed up, did his job, invested steadily, and raised a houseful of children. He did not start companies. He did not chase technology bets. He did not deplete his 401(k) to fund the next big idea. He did the boring thing.

Scott retired at forty.

Forty. While I was burning through every dollar I had saved to chase another startup, while I was ignoring every recommendation and every piece of advice anyone had ever given me in favor of risk, Scott Howell was free. He had time. He had options. He had the thing I was still swinging for.

I overcomplicated money my entire life the same way I overcomplicated connection.

After my first company failed, I spent five months drowning in alcohol and cigarettes. The relationship I had been in was over. The business was over. I was broke, directionless, and living the kind of life that looks romantic in a movie and pathetic in a mirror.

Then I got desperate. Desperate is underrated. Desperate people stop being clever and start being specific.

I went on Match.com. Instead of writing a charming introduction, instead of trying to cast a wide net and see what I caught, I did something that seemed insane at the time. I was specific. I wanted a woman within five miles. No pets. Speaks three languages. Plays two instruments. And absolutely loves Iron Maiden.

I married her six months later. She met every criterion.

Her name is Michele. She is Brazilian, from São Paulo. She speaks Portuguese, English, and Spanish. She plays piano and guitar. And she loves Iron Maiden. She was five miles away the entire time I was looking everywhere else.

If you search YouTube, "Iron Maiden Proposal," we are the only search result.

I tell you this because it is the same formula. The same principle that makes investing work, that makes choosing a freedom age work, that makes everything in this book work. Be specific. Pick a number. Define what you want with enough precision that the universe can actually deliver it. A vague wish produces vague results. A specific target produces specific outcomes.

My parents picked fifty-five. I picked fifty-five. I picked a woman who loves Iron Maiden. The specificity is the formula.

Just like my search for a wife, with investing I reached for sophistication before I mastered the obvious. I looked for secrets, shortcuts, or algorithms that could accelerate what cannot be accelerated. I assumed that because the outcome is significant, financial freedom, security, independence, the path must be equally complex.

It is not.

My worst financial decisions all involved real estate. I sold properties I did not need to sell. I moved because I wanted change, and change meant selling a house and buying a different one and losing money on the spread every time. I poured money into plaster boxes and convinced myself they were investments when they were really just expensive containers for restlessness.

I should have held. I should have played the long game. Index funds. Rental properties measured in decades, not moods. Compound interest doing its quiet, boring work. But I did not want quiet and boring. I wanted high-risk tech. I wanted the swing. And I got what big swings usually deliver.

Scott's Lowe's stock was not exciting. It was just right.

This is what we do when we are young. We try to rethink and reinvent. Questioning is in itself right. However, face value has more value than we think.

The wealth formula that works is boring. It is so boring that most people hear it, nod, and then go looking for something more interesting. They spend years searching for the better way, the faster way, the smarter way. Some of them find it. Most do not. And the people who simply followed the boring formula, year after year, decade after decade, ended up ahead of almost everyone who went looking for something clever.

This chapter is that formula. I will not dress it up. I will not make it exciting. Excitement is not the point. The point is that it works, and that it is available to almost anyone willing to be patient.

* * *

Choose Your Age

The formula begins before any account is opened, before any money is invested. It begins with a decision.

Choose an age. The age that you want complete freedom.

Not a vague intention to retire "someday" or "when I have enough." A specific number. Fifty-five. Fifty. Forty-eight. Sixty. The number matters less than the choosing. A chosen age becomes real in a way that "someday" never does.

Mine is fifty-five. My parents' number was also fifty-five. They put it on a license plate. I am putting it in a book. The difference is that this book includes the directions.

This is not because the number has magical properties. You may reach that age and decide to keep working. You may reach it and realize you need a few more years. You may reach it and discover you want to do something entirely different than you imagined. The number is not a prison. It is a compass. It sets the first marker of the rest of your life.

A vague future produces vague action. Believe me, I know this very well. I was without a plan and lived purely from hope and optimism. When retirement is "someday," every financial decision floats in uncertainty. Should I save more this month? Should I take this job? Should I buy this house? Without a target, these questions have no anchor. The answers drift toward whatever feels easiest in the moment.

A chosen age, a "freedom age," changes this. When retirement is "fifty-five," every decision can be measured against that target. Does this bring me closer or push me further away? The question becomes concrete. The math becomes possible. The daily choices accumulate toward something specific rather than dispersing into vagueness.

This quickly brings me to where we are with AI. Using a variety of applications, I can, in about fifteen seconds, tell you where I am in my journey. Can I survive a depression? Should we buy that thing or invest in that other thing? Technology exists to outline your plans, calculate your capacity, and give you the basis of informed decision making.

I am not asking you to predict the future, nor have your life planned by a bot. I am asking you to create a future worth planning for. The prediction may be wrong. The plan will certainly need adjustment. But the act of choosing, of saying "this is when I intend to be free," reorganizes how you think about time and money. You will use a number of tools, and more are on the horizon.

Most people never make this choice. They inherit the default age of sixty-five or whatever their country's pension system suggests, and they treat it as inevitable rather than chosen. But sixty-five is not a law of nature. It is a policy decision made by governments decades ago, based on life expectancies and economic conditions that no longer exist. You are not obligated to accept it. I am encouraging you to decide to live a second life. Live twice. The first half is when you earn and the second, you return. More on this later.

Choose your own number. Write it down. Tell someone. Make it real. Everything else follows from this.

* * *

The Boring Formula

The second part of the formula is equally simple, and equally ignored.

Open an investment account. Buy a basic index fund. Contribute a small amount every month. Automate it. Then forget it exists. This advice is so common it has become invisible. You have heard it before. You may have nodded and moved on. But hearing advice and acting on it are different things, and most people who hear this advice do not act.

So let me be direct and repetitive.

If you have a child, open an investment account for them as soon as you are able. In some countries, this will be a custodial account in your name until they reach adulthood. In others, it may be a junior investment account or the equivalent. The name does not matter. What matters is that the account exists and that money goes into it.

If you are reading this as a young adult, open an account for yourself. Today, if possible. This week, if not today. The account should be with a reputable brokerage, one that offers low-cost index funds and does not charge excessive fees. Most developed countries have several options. Ask someone you trust, or search for the most commonly recommended brokerages in your country. The information is not hidden.

If you are reading this at any age and do not yet have an investment account, open one. It is not too late. The best time to start was twenty years ago. The second best time is now.

Once the account exists, buy a broad index fund.

An index fund is a collection of stocks or other investments that tracks a market index, a broad measure of how the overall market is performing. In the United States, this might be a fund that tracks the S&P 500 or the total stock market. In Europe, it might track the STOXX Europe 600 or a global index. In Australia, the ASX 200. In the United Kingdom, the FTSE 100. The specific index matters less than the principle: you are buying a small piece of many companies rather than betting on any single one.

Why an index fund? Because it is simple, cheap, and almost impossible to beat over long periods. Decades of research have shown that most professional investors, people who spend their entire careers analyzing stocks, fail to outperform basic index funds over time. The fees they charge eat into returns. The trades they make often subtract value rather than add it. The index fund simply holds everything, charges almost nothing, and lets time do the work.

This is not exciting. It is not supposed to be. Excitement in investing usually costs money.

Once you own the index fund, contribute to it regularly. One hundred dollars a month, or one hundred euros, or the equivalent in your currency. If you can afford more, contribute more. If one hundred is too much right now, contribute fifty. The amount matters less than the consistency. The habit of regular contribution is what you are building.

Let me save you some math. With about one hundred dollars a month deposited for forty years, you will retire a millionaire. Now do the mental math if you wanted to retire faster. Twenty years. Ten years. Not the same outcome. Compounding rewards patience, not effort.

Automate the contribution so it happens without your involvement. Set it up once, then let it run. The money should leave your account before you have a chance to consider spending it elsewhere. This is not about discipline. Discipline fails eventually. This is about architecture. Build the system so that the right thing happens by default.

Then forget the account exists. Do not check it daily. Do not watch the market. Do not read articles about whether now is a good time to buy or sell. The answer to "is now a good time" is almost always "it does not matter if you are investing for decades." Short-term movements are noise. The signal is the long-term trend, and the long-term trend, over every period of several decades in modern market history, has been upward.

* * *

The Gift

I want to pause here and speak to what this account actually represents.

An investment account opened for a child at birth, funded with modest monthly contributions, will likely be worth a meaningful sum by the time that child reaches adulthood. Not because of any magic, but because of time. Twenty years of compounding, even on small amounts, produces results that feel disproportionate to the effort involved.

This single account, simple, boring, automated, can fund a wedding. It can provide a down payment on a home. It can seed a business. It can offer a young adult the rarest of gifts: options.

For decades, parents have been taught a narrow script for saving for their kids: 529 college plans, savings accounts, prepaid tuition, all wrapped in good intentions and tax incentives. The problem is that these tools assume a single outcome, college, on a fixed timeline, at an ever-inflating cost, and punish flexibility. Use the money for anything else and you are hit with penalties, taxes, or loss of control. Forget all those manufactured prisons.

They lock capital into a future that may not match the child's path, whether that's trade school, entrepreneurship, global work, or something that doesn't exist yet. The quiet truth is that the most valuable gift to a child isn't a perfectly optimized college account, but optionality: assets that can grow, adapt, and be deployed when the opportunity is clear, not when the account rules say it's allowed.

More importantly, this account teaches something that cannot be taught any other way. It teaches patience. It teaches that wealth is built slowly, not quickly. It teaches that investing is not trading, not gambling, not reacting to headlines. Investing is waiting.

A child who grows up knowing that an account exists in their name, growing quietly in the background, learns a different relationship with money than a child who does not. They learn that money can work for you while you sleep. They learn that time is an ally, not an enemy. They learn that the future is something you can prepare for, not just something that happens to you.

If you are a parent, this may be the most valuable financial gift you ever give your child. Not because of the money itself, but because of the lesson embedded in the money.

If you are a young adult reading this and your parents did not do this for you, that is not a moral failing on their part. They gave you what they knew to give. But you can do it for yourself now. You can open the account today and begin the process. Twenty years from now, you will be glad you did. More importantly, as a kid, you can direct the funds and buy stocks. My kids own Roblox, a game they play daily. They can see their account growing.

* * *

Boredom Is a Competitive Advantage

The hardest part of the formula is not starting. The hardest part is continuing without interference. Wealthy people actually talk about investing a lot.

Most people who invest do not fail because they chose the wrong fund or started at the wrong time. They fail because they cannot leave things alone. They check their accounts too often. They read too many articles. They hear that the market is about to crash, or about to soar, and they feel compelled to act. They sell when prices fall, locking in losses. They buy when prices rise, arriving late to gains. They trade and tinker and optimize, and each action, on average, makes things worse. They watch a movie, they read a new article or God forbid, Reddit. Advice is free, wisdom rarely is.

The data on this is overwhelming. The average investor earns significantly less than the funds they invest in, because they buy and sell at the wrong times. The fund might return eight percent over a decade, but the average investor in that fund earns five percent, or four, or less. The difference is behavior. The fund did fine. The investor could not sit still.

Waiting feels like doing nothing, which is why it is so difficult. We are trained to believe that effort produces results, that activity is virtuous, that the person who works hardest wins. In most areas of life, this is true. In investing, it is often the opposite. The person who does the least, who contributes regularly and then ignores the account for decades, tends to outperform the person who is constantly engaged.

The investor who can tolerate boredom, who can watch the market drop and shrug, who can read predictions of doom and do nothing, who can see others making quick profits and feel no envy, this investor will likely beat most of the people trying harder.

I understand that this is counterintuitive. It may even feel irresponsible, like I am advising you to be passive in an area that matters. But passivity here is not negligence. It is strategy. The strategy is to let compounding work without interruption. Every time you interfere, you risk breaking the chain.

There will be crashes. There will be years when your account loses twenty percent or more. There will be headlines screaming that this time is different, that the system is broken, that you must act now to protect yourself. These moments will feel urgent. They will feel like exceptions to the rule. They are not. They are the rule. Markets have always crashed and recovered. The crashes are part of the process, not interruptions to it.

If you sell during a crash, you turn a temporary decline into a permanent loss. If you wait, you allow the recovery to restore what was lost and continue building from there. This is not optimism. It is history. Every major market decline in modern history has eventually been followed by recovery and new highs. The only investors who were permanently harmed were those who sold at the bottom and never returned. Greed makes investors harm themselves by taking action on something that requires no action.

So, the formula includes this: when the crash comes, do nothing. Continue your regular contributions. Buy more at lower prices, if anything. Then wait. This is harder than it sounds, because fear is powerful and the urge to act will be strong. But the formula only works if you follow it through the difficult parts.

* * *

The Script of Other Societies

Switzerland taught me a valuable lesson. I lived there for two years as Chief Marketing Officer of two separate companies, and it was the first place that fundamentally changed how I thought about money and time.

Switzerland runs on a rigid script, and it doesn't apologize for it. Work early, save automatically, insure risks, invest conservatively, repeat. Every country has a formula, some accidental, some broken. Switzerland chose structure, and they got it right.

In my very first year, I accumulated roughly fifty thousand dollars in pension value without trying to be clever. It happened because the system assumes wealth-building is not optional. If I had stayed a decade, layered in raises and let compounding do its quiet work, the outcome was obvious long before retirement age.

What struck me most was how luxurious life felt for the average citizen. Not flashy wealth, but calm wealth. Clean cities, reliable infrastructure, real vacations, financial stability, and no constant low-grade panic about the future. Just as Asian cultures preserved physical capability by keeping the squat, Switzerland preserved financial capability by removing choice from the most important behaviors. Discipline was embedded, not debated.

The lesson is simple and uncomfortable: outcomes follow systems, not intentions. Bodies last longer when movement is unavoidable. Wealth grows when saving is unavoidable. When a culture gets the formula right, average people live extraordinary lives, not because they hustle harder, but because they align with a system that lets time work in their favor.

* * *

Free Money

For most people, the easiest way to build wealth is through their employment. This is not because jobs are noble or because employers are generous. It is because many employers offer retirement plans with matching contributions, and matching contributions are free money.

In the United States, this is often a 401(k). In the United Kingdom, a workplace pension. In Australia, superannuation. In Canada, an RRSP with employer matching. In Germany, a company pension scheme or Riester-Rente. The names differ, but the structure is often similar: you contribute a portion of your salary, your employer adds a matching contribution, and the combined amount grows tax-advantaged until retirement.

If your employer offers a matching contribution and you are not participating, you are declining free money. I do not use that phrase lightly. If your employer offers to match fifty percent of your contributions up to six percent of your salary, and you contribute six percent, your employer adds three percent. That is an immediate fifty percent return on your contribution, before any investment growth. No investment strategy in the world reliably produces fifty percent returns. The match does.

I understand that contributing to a retirement plan can feel impossible when money is tight. Every dollar that goes to the future is a dollar unavailable for the present, and the present has bills. But even small contributions, if matched, outperform larger contributions without matching. Contributing three percent and receiving a partial match may build more wealth than contributing six percent to an account with no match. The match changes the math.

If you are employed and your employer offers matching, find out the details. What percentage do they match? Up to what limit? What is the vesting schedule? Then contribute at least enough to capture the full match. If you can contribute more, do so. But at minimum, do not leave free money on the table.

If you are self-employed or your employer offers nothing, you will need to build the architecture yourself. This is harder but not impossible. Most countries have retirement vehicles available to the self-employed. In the United States, a Solo 401(k) or SEP-IRA. In the United Kingdom, a SIPP. In other countries, equivalent structures exist. The details vary, but the principle is the same: shelter what you can from taxes, invest in simple index funds, and let time work.

*   *   *

Taxes Are Real

Taxes cannot be avoided entirely, and attempting to avoid them entirely leads to places you do not want to go. But taxes can be managed. They can be deferred. They can be reduced through legal means.

The core insight is simple: most governments want you to save for retirement, because people who save are less likely to need government support later. To encourage saving, they offer tax advantages in two main forms. The first is tax deferral: you contribute before taxes, reducing your taxable income today, and pay when you withdraw in retirement. The second is tax-free growth: you contribute after taxes but the money grows and withdraws tax-free.

Right now, I have multiple 401(k)s, Roth IRAs, Simple and Traditional IRAs, and I don't know how to leverage them all. My accountant does though.

If taxes feel overwhelming or confusing, you are not alone. You do not need to master every detail. You need to understand that these accounts exist and that using them is better than not using them. The specific optimization can come later, or with the help of a professional. The first step is simply participating. You need the right person and I promise that person is out there.

One more thing about taxes: you do not eliminate them. You decide when you pay them. The government gets paid either way. Your decision is about timing and rate, not about escape. Understanding this removes some of the anxiety around tax planning. You are not trying to cheat the system. The rules exist to be used. Use them.

* * *

Five Hundred Thousand

Let me give you a number to hold in your mind: five hundred thousand.

Five hundred thousand dollars, or euros, or the rough equivalent in your currency. Half a million. This number is not magic, but it is meaningful.

For many people, five hundred thousand represents a threshold. Below it, you are still dependent: on your job, on circumstances, on the continued need to earn. Above it, something shifts. You are not free, necessarily. You may not be able to stop working entirely. But you have options you did not have before.

Five hundred thousand, invested reasonably, can generate twenty to twenty-five thousand per year in sustainable withdrawals. That is not luxury. In many places, it is not even comfortable. But it is a floor. It is the difference between "I must keep this job" and "I could survive without this job." It is the difference between fear and something closer to choice.

More importantly, five hundred thousand changes how risk feels. When you have nothing saved, every setback is a crisis. A job loss is an emergency. An unexpected expense is a catastrophe. You operate from scarcity, making decisions out of fear rather than consideration.

When you have five hundred thousand, the same setbacks hurt but do not destroy. A job loss is a problem to solve, not an existential threat. The cushion allows you to think clearly, to take time, to choose rather than react.

Here is the uncomfortable truth: five hundred thousand is achievable for ordinary earners. Not quickly. Not easily. But achievably. A person who invests five hundred dollars a month for twenty-five years, in a simple index fund earning average historical returns, will likely reach this threshold. The math is not complicated. It requires consistency, time, and the discipline to not interfere.

If five hundred is too much, start with two hundred. If two hundred is too much, start with one hundred. The exact amount matters less than the consistency and the time. The formula scales to what you can do, as long as you actually do it.

If I had known, I could have hit this number with sheer diligence when I was twenty-five. If I had been given the example shown in the spreadsheet, I could have seen retirement at thirty. That wasn't my number though.

*　*　*

Trust the System

This formula asks you to trust a system: financial markets, index funds, the continuation of economic growth, over periods of decades. That is a significant act of faith.

What I can say is this: the alternative to trusting the system is not safety. The alternative is trusting something else. Your ability to time markets. The predictions of experts. The stability of cash under your mattress. Each of these alternatives has its own risks, often larger than the risks of simple index fund investing.

Cash feels safe but loses value to inflation. Over decades, inflation can cut the purchasing power of cash in half or worse. Timing the market requires being right twice: knowing when to sell and when to buy back. Most people who attempt this fail. Even professionals mostly fail.

So yes, the formula asks you to trust a system. But the system it asks you to trust, diversified ownership of productive businesses across the economy, has a longer and more reliable track record than any alternative. It has survived world wars, depressions, pandemics, and countless predictions of imminent collapse. Betting against it is also a bet and, historically, a worse one.

* * *

The Index Card

I have now told you the formula. It is worth repeating, because repetition is part of how simple truths survive contact with complicated lives.

Choose a retirement age. A specific number. Write it down.

Open a brokerage account. Buy a basic index fund. Automate regular contributions. Then leave it alone.

If your employer offers a retirement plan with matching, participate. Capture the free money.

Use tax-advantaged accounts. Defer or reduce taxes legally.

Aim for five hundred thousand as the first meaningful threshold. Not because it is enough forever, but because crossing it changes everything.

Wait. Do not interfere. Do not react to headlines. Do not trade. Do not time the market. Wait.

That is the formula. It is simple enough to write on an index card. It is difficult enough that most people will not follow it. The difficulty is not intellectual. The difficulty is emotional. It requires patience when patience is boring. It requires stillness when action feels urgent. It requires faith in a process that offers no immediate feedback.

The formula works because it is boring enough to survive life. Exciting strategies require constant attention. They require good decisions made repeatedly under pressure. The boring formula requires almost nothing from you except consistency. It does not need you to be smart or lucky or attentive. It needs you to set it up once and then not destroy it. This is achievable. Not easy, but achievable. And achievable, sustained over decades, beats optimal-but-abandoned every time.

* * *

The Foundation, Not the House

There is one more thing the formula cannot do, and I want to be honest about it.

The formula cannot make you free by itself.

Five hundred thousand dollars, or a million, or any number you reach, provides options. It reduces fear. It creates a floor beneath you. But it does not, by itself, give you the life you want. It gives you the conditions under which that life becomes possible.

The person who accumulates wealth but has no idea what to do with freedom is not free. They are merely wealthy. They have solved one problem, the need to earn continuously, but they have not addressed the deeper questions: What do I actually want to do with my days? What gives my life meaning beyond work? Who am I when I am not defined by my job?

The formula in this chapter is necessary but not sufficient. It is the foundation, not the house. It creates possibility but does not fill that possibility with purpose.

This is why the chapters that follow matter. Accumulation alone is not the answer. The answer involves what you do with the optionality that accumulation provides. Remove the idea of "retirement" and introduce the concept of freedom. The complexity comes later. The beginning is boring, and that is exactly why it works.

For now, the task is simple. Begin. Open the account. Start the contributions. Choose the age. Let time work.

* * *

The Inversion

Here is something no financial advisor will tell you, because it would ruin their business model.

When you are making ends meet, you splurge. You get the bonus and you buy the thing you have been wanting. You try to impress. You earn excess and you spend it, because excess feels temporary and you want to taste it before it disappears.

But when you have freedom. When you have comfort and wealth of time. You spend less. Not because you are being disciplined. Because you do not want the same things anymore.

My t-shirts have no brands on them. I drive common, reliable cars. I do not want luxury items. I want luxurious experiences, once in a while. A meal in a place I have never been. A month in a country I cannot pronounce. A Tuesday with nothing on the calendar and no guilt about it.

The retirement fantasy is a beach house and a sports car. The retirement reality, the good version of it, is a blank Tuesday and a plain shirt.

* * *

I will quickly return to my mother, talking to the woman next to her in line. Sometimes it annoyed me so much.

She does not have a strategy. She does not have a system for building social capital. She simply does the small thing, over and over, and the accumulation takes care of itself. She speaks. She listens. She repeats. Over decades, this becomes a rich network of connection, built not through effort but through consistency.

If my mother has needs that I cannot provide, if she has some sort of issue and I am not there, she now has an army. An army of people that over time has compounded her value and returns that investment to her if she asks.

Building wealth works the same way. The formula is not clever. It does not require intelligence or insight or luck. It requires the willingness to do a small thing, over and over, for a long time. It requires trusting that accumulation works even when you cannot see it working. It requires patience with a process that offers no immediate gratification.

Most people who fail at building wealth do not fail because they lacked information. The information is everywhere. They fail because they could not sustain the boring thing long enough for it to matter. They got distracted. They got impatient. They went looking for something faster, something more exciting, something that felt more like action.

The formula survives because it asks so little of you. It does not require attention. It does not require decisions. It requires only that you set it up and then refrain from destroying it.

This is achievable. Not easy. Nothing about patience is easy. But achievable.

Begin now. The rest is waiting.

* * *

Questions Worth Sitting With

1. Can you do the boring thing and not overthink it? Not
   for a week, but for a decade? What makes that hard
   for you?

2. Who in your life inspired you to think differently about
   money, and where are they now? Did you follow their
   example or ignore it?

3. Who around you seems to carry no financial anxiety,
   and what do they do differently? Is their life simpler
   than yours, or just more intentional?

4. If you had to pick your freedom age right now, write it
   on a piece of paper, and tell someone, what number
   would you write? Why that number and not five years
   earlier?

5. When was the last time you were so specific about what
   you wanted that the universe had no choice but to
   deliver it?

CHAPTER 4

Optionality Changes Everything

"Security is mostly a superstition.
Life is either a daring adventure or nothing."
—Helen Keller

* * *

I once had a job I thought I loved. Good salary. Interesting work. Colleagues I respected. On paper, it was exactly what I was supposed to want. In fact, I moved to Switzerland because of it.

Then one Thursday afternoon, Boris Kraft, one of the founders of Magnolia, called me into his office and told me my position was being eliminated. Not because of performance. Not because of budget. Because I had completed my task. He was sorry. These things happen. I had two weeks. I had no family or friends nearby. No job prospects. A wife and two very small children.

I would not let go. I would fight and grip tighter than ever.

I refused to quit and told him that. I spent a weekend skiing alone in the Alps, thinking. Then I let go. We found a path forward and we are friends to this day.

Within a day of letting go, the universe gave me another opportunity just a few hours away. More money, more opportunity.

I had been holding something tightly, the need for that job to continue, the fear of what would happen if it didn't. I had not noticed how much energy that holding required until the thing I was holding was taken away.

The job felt like security. What it actually was, I understood now, was dependency dressed up as stability. I had one income, one path, one way my life could work. And as long as that path continued, I felt fine. But the fineness was fragile. It depended entirely on decisions made by people I would never meet in rooms I would never enter.

Since that time, I started thinking differently about security. Real security, I suspect, is not about finding the right job and holding on. It is about not needing any single thing so much that you forget what it is.

The previous chapters asked you to think about time and money. This chapter asks you to think about something more slippery: the feeling of freedom.

* * *

What Optionality Actually Is

Freedom is not a number. You do not wake up one morning with exactly enough money and suddenly feel free. Freedom arrives in layers. It comes from the gradual accumulation of options, ways your life could work that do not depend on any single path continuing.

Most of the stress people carry around money is not actually about money. It is about dependency. The person with one income and no savings is dependent on that income continuing. Every month, they must show up, perform, satisfy whoever controls their paycheck. If that relationship ends, everything ends. This is stressful not because the job is bad, but because the dependency is total.

The person with the same income but six months of savings is less dependent. They could survive a job loss. They could take time to find something better. They could say no to unreasonable demands without fearing immediate catastrophe. The job might be identical, but the experience of it is different. The fear is lower. The choices are clearer.

The person with multiple income streams, a job, a side project, some rental income, investments generating dividends, is less dependent still. No single source needs to continue for their life to work. They can lose one and survive on the others. They can walk away from something that no longer serves them. They can take risks that would terrify someone with only one path.

This is optionality. Not wealth, exactly. Not retirement. Just options. Ways your life could work. The more of them you have, the less any single one controls you.

* * *

Optionality Is Not Hustle

I want to be very clear about something, because it is easy to misunderstand.

The internet is full of advice about building multiple income streams, starting side businesses, monetizing your passions. Most of this advice comes wrapped in the language of grinding, optimizing, maximizing. Work your job, then come home and work your side hustle. Sleep less. Do more. Every hour is an opportunity to build.

This is exhausting. It is also counterproductive. The person who burns themselves out building a side business has not created optionality. They have created another obligation. They have traded one form of dependency for a more complicated form of dependency. Now they need both things to continue, and they are tired all the time.

Optionality should make your life lighter, not heavier. It should reduce stress, not add to it. If something you are building feels like a second job, if it exhausts you, if you dread it, if it leaves you with less energy for the things that matter, it is not creating optionality. It is creating burden.

The test is simple: Does this option make me feel more free or less free? If the answer is less, something is wrong. Either the option itself is wrong for you, or you are approaching it with the wrong mindset.

True optionality is reversible. You can stop. You can pause. You can let it sit for months and return to it later. If stopping would cause your life to collapse, it is not an option. It is an obligation with a different name.

Freedom does not come from grinding harder. It comes from needing less. Optionality is one way to need less, but only if the options themselves do not become new needs.

Good businesses give up on thousands of great ideas. Get good at giving up.

* * *

What You Already Know

The simplest forms of optionality come from skills you already have.

This is easy to overlook. We imagine that building income streams requires learning something new, developing expertise we do not possess, becoming someone different than we are. Sometimes that is true. But often, the fastest path to optionality is recognizing what you already know how to do, and letting other people pay you for it.

I discovered mine under pressure. The skill I had, the one I did not recognize as marketable for years, was creativity under stress. Given the pressure to survive or perform, I could find creative solutions to almost any business problem using technology and personal connections. I did not learn this in school. I learned it by nearly going broke repeatedly and having to invent my way out.

Every company I started required this. Easy Communities needed a technical solution I could not afford to buy, so I built one. Justice Pest Services needed customers I could not afford to advertise for, so I found them through relationships. Sparksight needed software that did not exist, so we wrote it from customer complaints. The skill was never the specific technology or the specific industry. The skill was the pattern: identify the problem, connect the people, build the thing, survive another month.

It took me years to realize that this pattern, this ability to solve business problems creatively under constraint, was what people would pay for. Not the code. Not the marketing. The thinking. The connections. The ability to walk into a room where no one knows what to do and leave with a plan that works. That was the skill. I had been giving it away for free inside my own companies for a decade before I understood it was the product.

I hate cars, my father loves them. You need not follow in the footsteps of anyone, including your parents, but you will need to find that person, not the thing, who gives you joy and inspiration.

You can do anything you want, but it's more fun to work with people who have the same passion.

Do what you love, then charge for it. Not as a mandate—not everyone needs to monetize their hobbies, and there is value in keeping some things purely for joy. But as an option. As a recognition that the things you do well, the things that come easily to you, are often the things others struggle with and will pay to have done.

The income from these efforts is often small. That is fine. Small income streams punch above their weight psychologically. A few hundred dollars a month from something you enjoy is not life-changing money. But it is proof of concept. It is evidence that you can generate income outside your main job. It is a crack in the wall of total dependency.

And sometimes, the small thing grows. Not always. Not usually. But sometimes what begins as a weekend hobby becomes something larger, something that generates real optionality, something that changes what is possible. You do not need to plan for this. You do not need to optimize for it. You just need to start, stay curious, and see what happens.

* * *

No One Really Cares

I want to pause here and offer some perspective. Because it is easy, in a chapter about optionality, to start feeling pressure. Pressure to build more options, to develop more income streams, to do more, more, more.

This would be a mistake. And it would miss the point.

Here is a truth that took me years to understand: no one really cares what you do.

I mean this in the most liberating possible way. The people around you, family, friends, colleagues, strangers, are not paying nearly as much attention to your choices as you imagine. They are busy with their own lives, their own worries, their own dramas. Your decision to start a side project or not start one, to invest in property or not invest, to pursue optionality or focus entirely on your main career, these decisions matter to you. They barely register for anyone else.

And yet. Despite the fact that no one is really paying attention, everyone still wants to tell you how to live. Your parents have opinions. Your friends have opinions. People you barely know will offer unsolicited advice about what you should do with your time and money. This is noise. Well-intentioned noise, often, but noise nonetheless. The people offering advice are not living your life. They are projecting their own fears and preferences onto you, because that is what humans do.

The Buddhist observation here is simple: much of your suffering is self-created. The pressure you feel to build optionality, to succeed, to have your life look a certain way . . . most of it exists only in your mind. You imagine others judging you. You imagine consequences that may never arrive. You create elaborate scenarios of failure and success, and then you react to those scenarios as if they were real.

Optionality helps with this. Not because it gives you more options, though it does. But because having options reduces the stakes. When you have multiple ways your life could work, no single path carries the weight of your entire future. You can try things without needing them to succeed. You can fail without being destroyed. The imaginary pressure loses its grip because the real consequences are smaller.

Most pressure is imagined. Options dissolve it.

✳   ✳   ✳

The Chain

So why does optionality change everything?

Not because it makes you rich. Optionality and wealth are related, but they are not the same thing. You can have significant wealth and very few options, locked into a job you cannot leave, a lifestyle you cannot afford to change. And you can have modest wealth but many options, ways to generate income, flexibility in how you live, freedom to choose.

Optionality changes everything because it changes fear.

Fear is the enemy of good decisions. When you are afraid of losing your job, of running out of money, of your life falling apart, you make decisions from a defensive crouch. You play not to lose rather than playing to win. You accept situations you should reject. You stay in places you should leave. You optimize for safety in ways that make you less safe over time.

For over twenty years, I lived in fear. Fear of debt. More debt.

When fear decreases, decisions improve. You can evaluate opportunities clearly, without the distortion of desperation. You can say no to things that do not serve you. You can take calculated risks, because the downside is survivable. You can think long-term, because you are not consumed by short-term survival.

Better decisions compound. The person who makes slightly better decisions, year after year, ends up in a dramatically different place than the person who makes slightly worse ones. Not because of any single choice, but because of the accumulated effect of thousands of choices, each one a little clearer, a little less distorted by fear.

Optionality. Lower fear. Better decisions. Compounding advantages.

This is the chain. Not optionality to wealth directly. Optionality to a way of moving through the world that tends to produce better outcomes over time.

* * *

I want to end this chapter by giving you permission to breathe.

The previous chapters were heavy. Time is running out. Money must be accumulated. Decisions must be made. These are true things, but they are also heavy things, and carrying heavy things is exhausting.

This chapter is meant to be lighter. Not because optionality is unimportant—it is very important, but because the path to optionality is not another form of grinding. It is not about working harder or doing more. It is about recognizing what you already have, building slowly on what you enjoy, and letting time do most of the work.

You do not need to have everything figured out. You do not need to build seven income streams by next year. You do not need to transform yourself into a different kind of person.

You need to start somewhere. Anywhere. A skill you already have that others might pay for. A relationship worth investing in. A small experiment worth trying. The starting matters more than the strategy. The doing matters more than the planning.

Freedom arrives in layers, not leaps. Each small option you create reduces your dependency by a fraction. Each reduction in dependency lowers your fear by a degree. Each degree of lower fear improves your decisions by a margin. The margins accumulate. The layers build. And one day, you realize that you are freer than you were, not because anything dramatic happened, but because small things accumulated into something significant.

The next chapter is about the people and the property. The specific stories of how optionality turned into freedom. Not theory. Names, numbers, and the lessons that cost real money to learn.

* * *

Questions Worth Sitting With

1. What are you holding so tightly right now that the grip itself is exhausting you? What would happen if you let go?

2. What skill do you already have, one you do without thinking, that other people would pay for if you offered it? Have you ever considered that the thing that comes easiest to you is the thing that is hardest for someone else?

3. If no one were watching and no one would ever know, what would you stop doing immediately? What does that answer tell you about how much of your life is performance?

4. Where in the world would you go next if money were irrelevant? What is actually stopping you from going? Is the barrier real or imagined?

5. What is the one thing you cherish more than anything that is not a person? Could you let go of it tomorrow and still be yourself?

CHAPTER 5

The People
and the Property

*"Community is the spirit, the guiding light, whereby
people come together to fulfill a purpose, to help others
fulfill their purpose, and to take care of one another."*

* * *

I mentioned earlier that I started a company called Sparksight. The story of how it began is less impressive than it might sound.

We grew quickly, but not because we were geniuses. We grew because we found good people, treated them well, and did work that was genuinely interesting. The company was barely profitable for years. We kept at it anyway, partly because we believed in what we were building, but mostly because we were having fun and did not know what else to do.

What we did know was that our customers had problems. They would tell us about them, not as formal requests, but as asides, frustrations, wishes. "We really need something that does X." "I wish there was a way to handle Y." We listened.

67

Over time, we started building small pieces of software to solve those problems. Not as products, exactly. As experiments. As responses to real needs, we had heard expressed by real people.

Those experiments accumulated. Some went nowhere. Some became tools we used internally. Some, over twenty years, became the foundations of businesses that made dozens of people millionaires. All because of one reason: recruiting.

I want to be careful here, because this could sound like a success story, and success stories are dangerous. They imply that if you just follow the right steps, you will arrive at the right destination. That is not how it works. What I want you to see is not the outcome but the process. We did not have a master plan. We had curiosity and persistence. We listened to customers and tried things. Most of the things did not work. A few did. The few that worked compounded over decades.

During those two decades, there were four major market crashes. Economic conditions that should have killed us. Moments when the rational thing to do was give up, cut losses, move on. We did not give up, for reasons that had less to do with strategy than with stubbornness and the fact that we were not paying attention to what the rational thing was supposed to be.

* * *

The Part That Isn't Flattering

Here is the part of the story that matters most, and it is not flattering to me.

Sparksight became truly successful after I left.

Not immediately after. But the trajectory changed when I was no longer in the middle of everything, making decisions, directing traffic, inserting myself into processes that worked better without me. I had hired good people. I had planted seeds that needed time and space to grow. What those seeds did not need was me, hovering over them, adjusting and optimizing and second-guessing.

Just like investing, I was the problem. My activity felt productive. My involvement felt necessary. But the company, like a portfolio, did better when I stopped interfering. My absence allowed it to grow in ways my presence had prevented.

This is a humbling thing to admit. We like to believe that our efforts are essential, that success flows from our involvement. Sometimes it does. But sometimes the most valuable thing we can do is step back, trust the systems we have built, and let compounding work without our interference.

Optionality, I learned, is not just about having options. It is about having the wisdom to let those options develop on their own.

* * *

Andy

The first customer Sparksight ever had was a man named Andy Meadows, Live Oak Interactive.

Andy was an entrepreneur, like me, but different in ways I did not fully appreciate until much later. He had more ideas than I did, and I had plenty of ideas. But more importantly, he had more patience. Where I was always chasing the next thing, eager for quick results, prone to boredom when progress felt slow, Andy was steady. He planted seeds and waited. He built relationships and let them mature. He understood, in a way I was still learning, that the best outcomes often come from doing less, not more.

If I was a day trader chasing GameStop, Andy was an index fund. While I was reacting to every headline, every opportunity, every shiny object that crossed my field of vision, Andy was quietly compounding. Not just money—relationships, knowledge, trust.

We stayed in touch after that first project. Over the years, when I did not know what to do, when I was stuck, or confused, or facing a decision I could not see clearly, I called Andy. Not for advice, exactly. More for perspective. He had a way of seeing situations that cut through the noise, that identified what actually mattered.

In 2016, I returned to the United States after a few years abroad and called Andy. The details are less important than the outcome: Andy made me wealthy. Not through some dramatic windfall, but through years of patient building that finally converted into something tangible. The optionality I had accumulated, the time I had invested in learning, the relationships I had maintained, the small experiments I had run, suddenly became real in a way they had not been before.

In 2025, he did it again.

I tell you this not to brag about outcomes. Outcomes are partly luck, and luck is not instructive. I tell you because financial freedom is not a strategy or a formula. It is a relationship.

A simple connection I made in 2006, selling services to a stranger who became a partner who became a friend.

The ability to pick a number, retire at fifty-five, did not come from my cleverness or my hustle. It came from a phone call I made when I did not know what to do, to someone who had more patience than me, who saw further than I could see, who understood things I was still learning.

Optionality is not just about income streams and side projects. It is about the people you know, the relationships you build, the trust you accumulate over decades. Andy's influence on my life was worth more than any investment I ever made. His ideas, his patience, his willingness to include me in things I would never have found on my own, these were the real options. Everything else was details.

* * *

Sticks and Stones

There is another form of optionality worth discussing, though I will approach it differently than most books do.

Real estate.

I am not going to write a real estate chapter. This is not that kind of book. But property deserves mention because it represents a particular kind of option, and because the way most people think about it is exactly backward.

Start with what property actually is. Strip away the emotion, the attachment, the sense that a building is somehow permanent or meaningful. What remains?

Sticks and stones.

A house is wooden sticks arranged in a pattern, with people living inside. A warehouse is metal sticks arranged differently, with stuff stored inside. An apartment building is stone and concrete, with people and stuff combined. That is all property is. Sticks and stones, configured for a purpose.

And here is what sticks and stones do: they decay. From the moment a structure is built, it begins falling apart. The roof degrades. The pipes corrode. The foundation settles. The wood rots or the metal rusts or the concrete cracks. Entropy is undefeated. Every building is in a slow race against its own deterioration.

So why does property appreciate? Not because of the sticks and stones, those are worth less every year. Property appreciates because of the place. The land. The location. The proximity to things people want to be near. The sticks and stones are incidental. They could be torn down and replaced, and the land would still be valuable.

Understanding this changes how you think about property. The building is not the asset. The building is a temporary configuration sitting on the asset. The land is what matters. The location is what appreciates. The structure is just along for the ride, slowly falling apart while the place beneath it becomes more or less desirable.

Most people treat property as precious. They buy a house, live in it, and hold it like a family heirloom. They become attached to the walls, the rooms, the memories accumulated there. They believe the property is worth what they feel it is worth, which is always more than the market might say, because feelings are not subject to market correction.

This attachment is understandable. Homes are where life happens. But attachment is the enemy of optionality.

If you believe your house is worth a million dollars, and someone else also believes it is worth a million dollars, sell it. Take the money. You have found a buyer who agrees with your assessment. This is rare and valuable. Do not wait for the ten-times return that real estate seminars promise. That return is not coming. It almost never comes. The people who achieved it bought in specific places at specific times, and their success is not a template. It is survivorship bias dressed up as strategy.

Sell when someone wants to buy. Rent it out if no one wants to buy yet. When that buyer appears, sell. Take the proceeds. Do it again if you want to, or deploy the capital elsewhere.

There is a Buddhist quality to good real estate thinking. Detachment, not indifference. You can care for a property, maintain it well, appreciate what it provides, while also recognizing that it is temporary, that its value is what someone will pay, that your attachment to it serves no one.

The sticks will rot. The stones will crack. The only question is whether you extract value before they do, or whether you hold on until the decay catches up with your beliefs.

* * *

The Dream House

We did this in 2025. I sold our dream house in Florida. The house I believed I would die in.

Bald eagles catching fish in the lake behind the house. Kids playing together every night till sunset. A pet alligator living three meters from our back door. My father had moved to Florida to be near us. Everything I thought I wanted was in that house or visible from its windows.

It stung. It hurt. I miss it.

However, I am glad it is sold.

The house was sticks and stones. The memories are mine. The eagles are still catching fish. The alligator does not know we left. And the freedom that selling created, the optionality it unlocked, was worth more than the attachment it replaced.

Detach. Transact. Move forward.

*   *   *

Choose Partners Like You Are Marrying Them

If you build anything, a side project, a business, an investment in property, you will likely do it with other people. Partners, co-founders, collaborators. And the choice of those people will matter more than almost any other choice you make.

I have learned this the hard way, and I have watched others learn it even harder.

Choosing a business partner is like choosing a spouse. You are binding yourself to another person, trusting them with your time, your money, your reputation. When it works, it is wonderful. The right partner multiplies your capabilities, compensates for your weaknesses, shares the burden when things get heavy. The best things I have built were built with partners I trusted completely.

When it does not work, it is catastrophic. A bad partner can destroy years of work. They can drain resources, damage relationships, make decisions that haunt you long after the partnership ends. And unlike a bad investment, which you can sell and move on from, a bad partnership is personal. It involves lawyers and accusations and the slow unwinding of something you built together.

The hardest part is that you often cannot tell the difference early on. Bad partners rarely announce themselves. They seem competent, aligned, trustworthy—until they are not. The problems emerge slowly, or all at once in a crisis, when it is too late to prevent the damage.

So, I will tell you what I wish someone had told me: vet partners like you are marrying them. Take time. Watch how they behave under pressure. See how they treat people who cannot help them. Ask hard questions about money, about values, about what happens when things go wrong. And if something feels off, if there is a hesitation you cannot name, a concern you cannot articulate, trust it. The cost of walking away from a questionable partnership is small. The cost of staying in one is enormous.

You can pivot ideas. You can abandon strategies that are not working. You can shut down businesses and start new ones. What you cannot pivot is character. The wrong person, chosen early, will cost you more than any bad idea ever could.

* * *

The next chapter is about life design. Not more money. Not more options. What to do with the freedom you are building. How to design a life worth retiring into, because retiring from something is only valuable if you are retiring to something.

But for now, rest here for a moment. You have absorbed a lot. The formula is in place. The options are beginning to form. What comes next is not more pressure.

What comes next is possibility.

* * *

Questions Worth Sitting With

1. Who in your life seems to never work yet always seems fine? What do they know about optionality that you haven't learned yet?
2. Who are the happiest people you know, and who are the people with the most interesting work? Are these the same people? If not, what does that tell you?
3. Have you ever watched something you built succeed without you? How did that feel? If you haven't, what does your inability to step away say about what you've actually built?
4. If you could call one person for perspective when you are stuck, not for advice but for clarity, who would it be? Have you told them what they mean to you?
5. What is your dream house? Now imagine selling it. What remains that the house was never responsible for?

CHAPTER 6

Designing a Life Worth Living

"The doctor of the future will give no medicine, but will instruct his patients in care of the human frame, in diet, and in the cause and prevention of disease."
—Thomas Edison

* * *

A tour of Asia that neither of us could afford eventually brought my friend Keith and I to Thailand, a land of harmonious contradictions: poverty and beauty, hedonism and deep spirituality, transactional objectification and genteel hospitality. Also, thousands of retired people, divorced men, and young hooligans. Many lessons there.

We toured dozens of temples, listening to the resonant voices of monks chanting sutra, standing in awe at gold-leaf covered Buddhas and stupas. This trip changed me, made me more spiritual than my Baptist upbringing ever did. Eventually, we landed in the west-facing city of Pattaya, perfectly situated on the eastern shore of the Gulf of Thailand.

It was there we were walking along the gulf at sunset, truly the golden hour where the light forgives everything. Keith, a writer and technologist, and I were doing what men do best in that light: solving the world's problems with absolute confidence and zero implementation plans.

Then I saw him.

A lone stray dog, seated perfectly on the beach, facing away from us. The sun poured gold onto his muzzle. He stared into the horizon like a monk who had already finished the book. Noble. Regal. Content. This dog knew who he was. He needed nothing. He was alone, and always would be. A philosopher king with fleas.

I stood there silently, letting the meaning of existence gently rearrange itself inside me.

"What are you looking at?" Keith asked.

"That dog. It came down to this beach to sit by itself and take in the sunset. It's amazing."

Keith has always been a pragmatist. Stoic. Prone to anhedonia. Hesitant to let loose—which is one of the reasons I had organized this trip, to try and bring him some level of visible happiness.

He chuckled at my observation. "But he's not alone," he said, gesturing. As we continued to walk and the small rise in sand moved out of view, sure enough, there were several other dogs there. Some sleeping. Some self-grooming.

Where I had seen an enlightened wolf-king and felt a surge of situational enlightenment, Keith saw a pack of ragged street dogs, quite common in Southeast Asia. Whereas I had anthropomorphized the one dog into a kind of guru, Keith understood that these dogs were hanging out where humans, and their food, hung out.

Keith laughed. Loudly. The universe, which had expanded into focus for me only moments before, snapped shut. And just like that, my deep spiritual revelation was downgraded to a very nicely lit coincidence.

I had seen something in a different way. Then someone externally ruined it. They told me how to see something, and I listened.

That is how most people approach the years after work. They have been told to see it in a specific way, as decline, as ending, as the slow fade to irrelevance, and they laugh at anyone who looks at it differently.

This chapter is about seeing it differently. Not retirement. Not ending. A second life, and what your body needs to be capable of living it.

* * *

What Does a Good Day Look Like?

There is a quiet question that money cannot answer, no matter how much of it you accumulate.

What does a good day actually look like?

Not a vacation day. Not a special occasion. An ordinary day.

A Tuesday in March. A Thursday in September. The kind of day that makes up most of a life, the kind that passes without ceremony or memory.

What would that day contain, if you could design it freely? What time would you wake? What would you do in the morning hours, when energy is highest? Who would you see? What would you make, or learn, or experience? How would the afternoon unfold? The evening? What would leave you, at the end of that day, feeling that it was well spent?

Most people have never seriously considered this question. They have thought about goals, achievements they want to reach, possessions they want to acquire, milestones they want to pass. But goals are not days. You can achieve every goal you set and still spend most of your days feeling vaguely dissatisfied, because the days themselves were never designed. They just happened, one after another, shaped by defaults and obligations rather than intention.

The person who knows what a good day looks like has something most people lack. They have a template. Not a rigid schedule, not a productivity system, but a sense of what kinds of activities and interactions and rhythms leave them feeling alive. When freedom arrives, they know how to fill it. The space that freedom creates has something to flow into.

The person who does not know what a good day looks like has only the space. And space without form is not freedom. It is disorientation.

Life design does not begin when you stop working. It begins now. It begins whenever you start paying attention.

* * *

The Enabler

None of this matters if your health fails.

I am not going to give you a wellness program. There are enough books about diet and exercise and sleep, written by people more qualified than me. What I want to say is simpler: health is the enabler of choice.

Every option you build—financial, professional, personal—depends on having a body and mind capable of exercising those options. The money means nothing if you cannot move. The freedom means nothing if you cannot think clearly. The relationships mean nothing if you cannot show up for them.

This is obvious, and yet it is constantly neglected. We defer health the same way we defer life design. We tell ourselves we will get serious about it later, after this project, after this deadline, after we have more time. We treat our bodies as infinitely tolerant, as if the accumulated neglect will never come due.

It comes due. Not always dramatically, not always suddenly, but inevitably. The body keeps a ledger. The decades of sitting, of stress, of poor sleep, of food chosen for convenience rather than nourishment, they accumulate. And the bill arrives, usually around the same time you finally have the freedom to live differently.

The second life you are building requires a body capable of living it. The choices you make at thirty-five affect what is available to you at sixty-five. Those choices are not just about longevity, living longer, but about capacity. The ability to do things. To move through the world. To show up fully for the life you have designed.

* * *

The Tax That Increases

There is a specific thing I want to mention, because almost no one talks about it honestly.

Alcohol.

I am not going to lecture you. I am not going to tell you to stop drinking or to feel guilty about enjoying a glass of wine. What I am going to tell you is what your body already knows, even if you have not been listening.

The drink that cost you nothing at twenty-eight costs you something at forty-eight. The same drink. The same amount. Different price.

In your twenties and thirties, alcohol is mostly fun. Your body processes it efficiently. You wake up the next morning a little tired, maybe, but functional. The cost to your productivity, your clarity, your energy, it is low enough to ignore. So you ignore it.

Somewhere in your forties, the math changes. The same two glasses of wine that once meant nothing now mean a foggy morning. The night out with friends now costs you the next day, sometimes two days. Recovery takes longer. Sleep, already harder to come by, becomes even more disrupted. The fun remains, but the tax increases.

I learned this personally. When I moved to Portugal at fifty-four, I discovered wine that cost two euros a bottle. Exceptional wine. I drank it at lunch and dinner for six months. When that stopped working, it became hard liquor and a beer. I was on vacation, I told myself. I was relaxing into my new life.

Then I started noticing patterns. Not in myself at first, in the people around me. The expats who had relocated for the lifestyle but looked ten years older than their age. The retirees whose afternoons started with "just one glass" and ended with them shuffling home. The brilliant people whose brilliance had gone fuzzy around the edges.

I saw the same pattern in artists and executives and writers I admired. The ones who lasted, who stayed sharp into their seventies and eighties, had all reached a point of reconciliation. They understood that certain things hurt you at certain ages. They adjusted. Not with deprivation, but with honesty.

The reconciliation is simple, if uncomfortable: the things you got away with when you were young, you will not get away with forever. The cost of each increases with age. This is not punishment. It is physics. The machine wears differently at different stages of use.

You do not have to be perfect. But you do have to be honest. The body that will carry you through your second life is being shaped by the choices you make now.

* * *

The Data

Here is something that would have seemed like science fiction twenty years ago: I know when I am getting sick before I feel sick.

I wear an Oura ring that tracks my sleep, my heart rate variability, my body temperature. I have a Withings scale that measures not just weight but body composition, heart health, and vascular age. A blood pressure monitor that logs every reading to my phone. An Apple Watch that tracks my movement, my workouts, my irregular heartbeats.

Every morning, I check my Readiness score. It is a number that synthesizes all this data into a simple question: how prepared is your body for the day ahead?

When my Readiness is high, I make decisions. I take meetings. I buy things. I say yes to opportunities.

When my Readiness is low, I do none of that. I have learned, through expensive mistakes, that decisions made on low-Readiness days are almost always regretted. The deal that seemed urgent was not. The purchase that felt necessary sits unused. The commitment I made became a burden I resented.

This sounds obsessive. It is not. It takes two minutes a day. And it has fundamentally changed how I move through life.

The data does not make decisions for me. It gives me information I did not have before. I know when my body is fighting something before symptoms appear. I know when my sleep debt is accumulating. I know when I need to rest and when I can push. I am not guessing. I am not relying on how I feel, which is notoriously unreliable. I have data.

This matters for your second life because the margin for error shrinks as you age. At thirty, you can override bad data, power through fatigue, ignore warning signs, recover quickly from poor decisions. At sixty, you cannot. The body that once forgave everything now remembers everything. Knowing what state you are in becomes the difference between sustainable freedom and preventable decline.

* * *

Geography Is a Financial Strategy

Now here is something that changes every calculation you have made about healthcare: it does not cost the same everywhere.

Americans treat healthcare costs as fixed, as if the price of a procedure or a medication is determined by some universal law. It is not. It is determined by where you are standing when you need it.

In Portugal, where I live, my annual healthcare costs for a family of four are nine hundred dollars. Not nine hundred a month. Nine hundred a year. That includes coverage that would cost ten times as much in the United States.

A heart stent, if I needed one, would cost fifty-nine dollars. Not fifty-nine thousand. Fifty-nine.

The care is not inferior. The doctors are not less qualified. The hospitals are not worse equipped. The difference is the system, how healthcare is structured, funded, and priced. The same procedure, the same outcome, radically different cost depending on which side of an invisible line you happen to be standing on.

This matters for your second life because healthcare costs are one of the primary reasons people delay freedom. They stay in jobs they hate because of the insurance. They defer living because they are terrified of a medical catastrophe. They calculate their freedom number based on American healthcare costs and conclude they cannot afford to stop.

But if you are willing to live abroad, even part of the year, that calculation changes completely. The prison you thought you were in has a door you did not notice.

I am not saying everyone should move to Portugal. I am saying that healthcare is a variable, not a constant. Part of designing your second life is understanding that the costs you assume are fixed may not be fixed at all. Geography is a financial strategy.

* * *

The Rules Are About to Change

There is another reason to pay attention to your health now, and it has nothing to do with discipline or willpower or avoiding regret.

The rules are about to change.

Artificial intelligence is advancing healthcare at a rate never before seen in human history. Not incrementally. Exponentially. The diagnostic tools, the drug discovery pipelines, the personalized treatment protocols, all of it is accelerating faster than most people realize.

Within the next decade, we will have the ability to detect diseases years before symptoms appear. Not through intuition or luck, but through AI systems analyzing patterns in data that no human could process. Cancers caught at stage zero. Heart conditions identified from voice recordings. Alzheimer's predicted from eye movements.

We will have drugs developed in months instead of decades. Treatments tailored to your specific genetic profile. Interventions that repair damage we currently consider irreversible.

I am not predicting utopia. There will be problems: access, cost, inequality, unintended consequences. But the direction is clear: we are entering an era where the limits of human health are going to expand dramatically.

What this means for your second life is simple: you may have more years than you think. The assumptions built into traditional retirement planning, that healthspan ends around seventy-five, that decline is inevitable and predictable, may not hold. Someone reading this book at thirty might reasonably expect to live with quality into their nineties or beyond.

This is not a reason to delay freedom. It is a reason to protect your health now, so you are positioned to benefit from what is coming. The people who maintain their bodies through the next two decades will have options that the people who do not will not have. The future will reward those who arrive at it in good condition.

Your second life may be longer than any generation before you could imagine. Design accordingly.

* * *

Pay Attention to the Margins

Life design sounds grand. In practice, it is modest.

It is the slow accumulation of self-knowledge. It is paying attention to what you enjoy and what drains you. It is noticing who you want to spend time with and who you endure out of habit. It is the willingness to adjust when something is not working. It is the recognition that you are the only one who can know what a good day looks like for you, and that finding out is not a problem to solve but a life to live.

The question of what a good day looks like is not a question you answer once and file away. It evolves. The good day you wanted at thirty is not the good day you want at fifty. The activities that energized you in one phase of life may bore you in another. Life design is continuous, iterative, always in draft.

What I can tell you is this: pay attention to the margins. The early mornings, the evenings, the weekends, the time that is actually yours, not claimed by work or obligation. How you spend those margins reveals something important. It reveals what you reach for when reaching is optional.

Some people fill their margins with activity: projects, hobbies, socializing. Some fill them with stillness: reading, walking, simply being. Neither is wrong. But if you have never noticed what you do with unstructured time, you do not yet know yourself well enough to design a life around that self.

The freedom you are building will create space. What you put in that space is up to you. The margins are where you practice. Pay attention to them, and the answers you need will emerge.

* * *

I want to give you permission to approach this lightly.

Life design can become another form of optimization, another source of pressure, another way to feel like you are falling behind. It should not be. The goal is not to architect a perfect second life before you arrive at it. The goal is to arrive with enough self-knowledge that you can navigate it.

You do not need a plan. You need attention. Attention to what you enjoy. Attention to who you enjoy being with. Attention to the rhythms and activities that leave you feeling alive. The data is all around you, generated by your own experience. The only requirement is that you notice it.

My friend who went to Thailand with me, the pragmatist who saw the street dogs, eventually found his own second life. It looks nothing like mine. He is not in Portugal drinking two-euro wine. He is in Texas, building things, still working but on his terms. His good day is not my good day. It does not need to be.

You will find your way too. Not by planning harder, but by paying attention. Not by knowing in advance, but by learning as you go.

The freedom you are building will create space. What you put in that space is up to you.

There is no rush. There is only the invitation to notice. And to take care of the body that will carry you there.

The next chapter is about what to do with that space once you have it. Not retirement, that word carries too much baggage. What we are building is a second life. A new beginning that happens to come after the first one. The removal of obligation, with everything that remains still possible.

*　*　*

Questions Worth Sitting With

1. Do you measure any part of your health with actual data? If your body sent you a daily readiness score, what would it say this morning?

2. If you could look at your family health history, your habits, and the actuarial tables, and pick the age you think you might die, what age would you choose? Now subtract twenty years. That is roughly where your healthspan ends. How does that change your planning?

3. What does a genuinely good Tuesday look like for you? Not a vacation. Not a celebration. An ordinary day, designed by you, with nothing on the calendar you didn't choose.

4. What are you still getting away with, a habit, a substance, a pattern, that has an expiration date you haven't acknowledged?

5. When you have unstructured time, no meetings, no deadlines, no obligations, what do you reach for? That answer reveals more about who you are than any goal you've ever set.

CHAPTER 7

Building Your Second Life

*"Guard well your spare moments. They are like
uncut diamonds. Discard them and their
value will never be known."*
—Ralph Waldo Emerson

* * *

If you want to understand what comes after work in America,
go to Florida.

Not the Florida of Miami Beach or Palm Beach, where wealth
concentrates in towers overlooking water. The other Florida.
The Florida where the second life actually happens, in trailer
parks with palm trees out front, plastic flamingos in the yard,
and mortgage payments that cost less than your cable bill.

Florida is the melting pot of the post-work life, the place
where every version of it comes to simmer in the same humid
soup. And what a soup it is.

There is the weather, of course. Perpetual summer. Winter is a rumor, something that happens to other people in other states. Life is scheduled around air-conditioning maintenance, golf carts, and the afternoon thunderstorms that arrive like clockwork. Sunscreen becomes a food group. The sun—relentless and democratic—bakes everyone equally, the wealthy and the modest, the planners and the drifters.

There is the tax situation. No state income tax. No inheritance tax. Florida has structured itself as a fiscal paradise for people in the final chapters, because nothing says life planning like dying efficiently. The state has made a business model of attracting people who have spent decades paying taxes elsewhere and now wish to stop.

There is real estate, spanning every possible price point. Beachfront condos worth millions. Gated communities with golf courses and clubhouses. And trailers, endless trailers, arranged in communities with names like "Paradise Palms" and "Sunset Village," where people live full lives on Social Security checks and the understanding that a home does not need to be expensive to be enough. You can buy a fully furnished four-bedroom trailer with a lake view for around twenty thousand dollars. The flamingos are plastic. The alligators are not. This is important to remember.

There is the wildlife, which refuses to respect the boundaries humans have drawn. Alligators in the retention ponds. Iguanas on the sidewalks. Manatees in the canals. People navigate this landscape in golf carts, moving between the clubhouse and the grocery store, sharing the roads with creatures that were here long before the first trailer was parked. Everyone pretends this is completely normal, because in Florida, it is.

And there is—I mention this because it exists and says something important—the optional clothing lifestyle. Nude beaches. Nudist resorts. Communities where people live entirely naked, proving that gravity is undefeated and confidence is tax-free. They play shuffleboard without clothes. They garden without clothes. They have accepted something about the human body that the rest of us are still negotiating, namely, that clothing is optional, but sunscreen is mandatory.

I describe all of this not to mock it. I describe it because Florida contains every possible answer to the question of what the second life can look like. The wealthy and the working-class. The active and the sedentary. The clothed and the unclothed. The planned and the improvised. All of them, living side by side, sharing the same sunshine and the same hurricanes. No one cares what you look like or what you have.

No matter how you live, you can live in Florida. With something or with nothing. In a mansion or a trailer. Dressed or undressed. The state does not judge. It simply offers the weather and the tax breaks—and lets people figure out the rest.

My father lives in a trailer in Florida now. Works part-time as a security guard at a nudist resort. I could not have written that sentence ten years ago. I could not have imagined it.

But here's the thing: he found people to talk to, a reason to leave the house, and a job where the dress code is, technically, optional. He stopped waiting for the script to tell him what to do and started improvising. For the record, the lunch at the resort is great and the poolside band is awesome.

I'm proud of him. He lives and works where he has a view.

And here is what Florida reveals, if you pay attention: the second life is not one thing. It is not a single lifestyle or a single income level or a single way of spending your days. It is a space, a removal of certain constraints, that people fill in radically different ways. The person in the beachfront condo and the person in the trailer park have something in common. They are both done being told what to do. Everything else is details.

*   *   *

Your Second Life Begins When Obligation Ends

The cultural image of what happens after work is a slow fade to irrelevance. You work, you contribute, you matter. Then one day, you stop. You hand in your badge or your keys or your title, and you cross an invisible line. On the other side of that line, you are no longer a participant. You are an observer.

This image is pervasive. It shapes how we talk about the end of careers, as an ending, a withdrawal, a stepping back. It shapes the fear that many people carry, often unspoken: the fear that leaving work means becoming invisible, unnecessary, obsolete.

This fear is not irrational. Many people do experience their post-work years as decline. They leave their jobs and discover they have nothing to replace them with. Their social connections evaporate. Their sense of purpose disappears.

But the image is also a choice. It is one way the transition can go, not the only way.

Let me offer a different definition.

Your second life begins when obligation ends.

Not when work ends. You may keep working, if you choose. Not when income ends. You may keep earning. Not when contribution ends. You may contribute more than ever. Just when obligation ends. When the things you *must* do become the things you *might* do. When the schedule imposed by others becomes a schedule you choose.

You can retire as many times as you want, at any age you want. The word "retire" just means removing the obligation. You can remove it at thirty-five and add it back at forty. You can remove it at fifty-five and discover you miss it and return. The door swings both ways. The only thing that changes is who is holding the handle.

* * *

Identity Evolves

The fear of losing identity is real, and it deserves to be taken seriously.

For decades, you have been something. A teacher, an engineer, a manager, a salesperson. The role shaped your days, your relationships, your sense of self. When someone asked who you are, you had an answer. The answer was not complete, you were always more than your job, but it was stable. It located you in the world.

Leaving work removes the answer. Or rather, it removes the easy answer. You are no longer the thing you did. The title is gone. The role is gone. The daily confirmation of your place in the world is gone. What remains is a harder question: who are you, underneath the job?

But here is what I want you to understand: identity does not disappear when obligation is removed. It evolves.

The identity you built around work was real, but it was also constrained. It was shaped by what employers wanted, what the market rewarded, what was available to you at the time. When obligation is removed, the constraints lift. You are free to explore parts of yourself that work suppressed. You are free to develop skills that had no market value. You are free to become someone you could not become while the job was defining you.

This is why I call it a second life, not an ending. It is a rebirth. Not into a different person, but into a fuller version of yourself. The parts that were dormant can wake up. The interests that were deferred can surface.

The discomfort of transition is real. Expect it. Sit with it. But do not mistake it for evidence that you have made a mistake. The discomfort is the feeling of identity reorganizing itself. It passes. What remains, if you let it, is a larger sense of who you are.

* * *

The Comparison Trap

Envy is one of the most corrosive emotions available to humans. It distorts perception. It poisons relationships. It makes other people's success feel like your failure. And it has a particular power over decisions about work and life transitions.

The person who is ready to leave but watches a peer continue climbing the ladder feels the pull of comparison. Why are they still going? What do they know that I do not? Am I giving up too early?

The person who has already transitioned but sees former colleagues achieving new successes feels comparison differently. It arrives as regret, as doubt, as the quiet suggestion that perhaps they made a mistake.

The antidote is not to stop noticing others. That is impossible. The antidote is to notice the noticing. To catch yourself in the act of comparison and ask: is this relevant? Does that person's choice tell me anything about my own situation? Or am I importing their values, their goals, their definition of success into a life where those things do not apply?

Your second life is not a comment on anyone else's choices. Their continued work is not a comment on yours. The comparison game has no winner. The only way to win is to stop playing.

* * *

Stuff

There is another weight that keeps people tied to obligation longer than necessary, and it accumulates so gradually that most people do not notice it.

Stuff.

Every possession you own carries a cost. Not just the purchase price, but the ongoing cost of housing it, maintaining it, insuring it, thinking about it. A larger house requires more furniture, which requires more cleaning, which requires more time or more money to hire help. Each addition to your life adds mass. And mass requires energy to maintain.

The person who lives simply, not miserably, not ascetically, but simply, needs less to be free. Their threshold for enough is lower. They can remove the obligation sooner, because the obligation was smaller to begin with.

There is also the question of what the stuff represents. Much consumption is not about the thing itself. It is about what the thing signals. The label on the clothing, the brand of the car, the address of the house. These are status markers, purchased to communicate something about who you are.

Here is a thought worth sitting with: if you wear a label, someone else got rich first. The premium you paid for the logo went to shareholders, to executives, to the company that convinced you the label matters. You purchased the right to advertise for someone else. The status you sought enriched others before it signaled anything about you.

Simplicity is not virtue. It is strategy. The lighter your life, the easier it is to move. The less you need, the sooner you can stop needing to earn. Stuff and freedom exist in tension. Choose accordingly.

*   *   *

Money Is Not the Enemy

I want to say something about money that may sound strange.

Money is not the enemy.

Many people develop an adversarial relationship with money. They fear it. They resent the need for it. They feel ashamed of wanting it or guilty for having it. Money becomes a source of anxiety rather than a tool for building the life they want.

This attitude is counterproductive. Money does not care how you feel about it. Your fear does not make it go away. Your resentment does not reduce your need for it.

Money is a relationship, and like all relationships, it works better with calm attention than with fear or avoidance.

The person who fears money makes poor decisions. They

avoid looking at their accounts because looking is uncomfortable. They defer planning because planning forces confrontation. They stay in jobs they hate because the job provides money, and money is too scary to think about clearly.

The person who approaches money calmly makes better decisions. They know what they have. They know what they need. They can calculate, without panic, whether their situation is stable.

Developing a calm, positive attitude toward money is part of the work of building your second life. Money is a tool. Like all tools, it serves the person who understands it and frustrates the person who fears it. Your freedom depends on this tool working properly. That requires attention, not avoidance. Respect, not resentment.

* * *

Optional Work

Here is something that surprises people who have never met someone living their second life.

Most of them work.

Not full-time. Not for the money. Not because they have to. But they work. They consult a few hours a week. They teach a class. They serve on a board. They help a friend's business. They write…or build…or create things that sometimes generate income and sometimes do not.

This confuses people who think leaving your career means stopping. If you are still working, how can you be in your second life?

The answer is in the word "obligation."

A person in their second life who works is not obligated to work. They could stop tomorrow, and their life would continue. The money from the work is welcome but not necessary. The work itself is chosen, not imposed. If it stops being interesting, they stop doing it. If something better comes along, they pursue that instead.

Optional work feels lighter. This is not imagination. It is physics. The weight of obligation is real. When you carry something because you must, it presses down. When you carry something because you want to, the same weight feels different. The task may be identical. The experience is not.

Many people in their second life report that they enjoy work more than they ever did before. This sounds paradoxical until you understand the shift. They are doing similar activities, but without the pressure. The work that felt like burden now feels like choice. The same hours, the same tasks, somehow transformed by the removal of must.

Your second life does not mean you will never work again. It means you will never be forced to work again. What you do with that freedom, including whether you continue working, is up to you.

*   *   *

I began this chapter with Florida, where every possible version of the post-work life exists side by side.

The person in the mansion and the person in the trailer. The one playing golf every day and the one gardening naked. The one who moved there to be near grandchildren and the one who moved to escape them. All of them, different as they are, share something: they are no longer being told what to do.

That is the common thread. That is what the second life actually is. Not a particular lifestyle. Not a particular income. Not a particular way of spending your days. Just the removal of external compulsion. The freedom to choose.

The only wrong choice is to never make one. To stay in obligation forever because you are afraid of what comes after. To assume that leaving work means leaving life, when the opposite is often true.

You do not need to disappear. You just need to stop being forced.

The final chapter is not about more planning. It is about arrival. About what it feels like when the obligation finally lifts. About the morning when you wake up and realize that the weight you carried so long has been set down.

That morning is closer than you think.

✳ ✳ ✳

Questions Worth Sitting With

1. If you had nothing to do tomorrow and no one to report to, how would you spend the day? Be specific. Hour by hour. If you cannot answer this, that is the problem this chapter is about.

2. What part of your identity is your job? If someone asked "who are you" and you could not mention your title, your company, or your industry, what would you say?

3. If you could meet anyone in the world for coffee or tea, who would it be, and where? What would you ask them? What do you think they would ask you?

4. Do you feel weighed down by things? Possessions, obligations, relationships maintained out of habit rather than choice? What would your life feel like if you cut the weight in half?

5. What is the difference between retiring from something and retiring to something? Which one scares you more?

CHAPTER 8

Arrival

*"The meaning of life is just to be alive. It is so plain
and so obvious and so simple. And yet, everybody
rushes around in a great panic as if it were necessary
to achieve something beyond themselves."*
— Alan Watts

* * *

There is a morning that arrives without announcement.

You wake up, and something is different. Not the room, not
the light, not the circumstances of your life. Something quieter
than that. Something in the quality of the waking itself.

The alarm did not go off, because there is no alarm. The day
ahead contains nothing that must happen at a particular time.
You lie there for a moment, aware of the ceiling, aware of the
light shifting, aware of your own breathing. And you notice that
the weight you have carried for years, so familiar you had forgotten it was there, has lifted.

This is not excitement. Excitement is loud, forward-leaning, hungry for what comes next. This is something else. This is the absence of urgency. The day feels open rather than empty. The hours ahead are not a void to be filled or a problem to be solved. They are simply available. Yours.

You get up slowly. You make coffee. You stand at a window or sit on a porch or simply pause in your kitchen, and you notice that you are not thinking about what you should be doing. You are not calculating. You are not rehearsing the tasks ahead or reviewing the tasks behind. You are just there, in that moment, with the coffee and the light and the quiet.

This is what freedom feels like. Not loud. Not dramatic. Not the fireworks and champagne of achievement. Just this. A morning without pressure. A day without demand. The simple, unremarkable experience of being present in your own life.

* * *

Others Notice

Other people notice before you fully understand what has changed.

They see something in your face, your posture, the way you move through a room. You seem lighter, they say. More relaxed. They cannot identify what shifted, but they can feel its effects. You laugh more easily. You listen more fully. You are not always glancing at your phone or checking the time or calculating how long until you need to be somewhere else.

Some of them are curious. They want to understand. They lean in, ask more, wonder if what you have found is available to them too. These conversations are easy. You share what you can, knowing that the path is different for everyone, that what worked for you may not work for them, that the most you can offer is description, not prescription.

Others are unsettled in a different way. Your calm reflects something back to them that they do not want to see. If peace is possible, why don't they have it? If freedom is achievable, why are they still trapped? Your presence becomes an accusation, even though you have accused no one. They may pull away, or criticize, or explain why what you have done would never work for them. This is not about you. It is about the stories they are telling themselves.

You learn to hold all of this lightly. The curiosity and the discomfort. The questions and the deflections. None of it changes what you have found. Peace does not require agreement. Contentment does not need witnesses.

* * *

The Need to Explain Fades

There was a time when you would have explained. You would have justified your choices, defended your path, offered evidence and arguments for why this way of living makes sense. You would have wanted others to understand, to approve, perhaps even to follow.

That impulse fades.

Not because explanation is wrong, but because it is unnecessary. The life you are living is its own justification. It does not require external validation. It does not need to be right in any-one else's framework. It simply needs to be yours.

This is a strange kind of freedom, the freedom from needing to be understood. For years, you sought approval, from parents, from employers, from society at large. You made choices partly based on how they would be perceived. You optimized not just for outcomes but for the story the outcomes would tell.

Now the audience has thinned. Not because people have stopped watching, they watch as much as ever, but because you have stopped performing. The choices you make are not for them. The life you are building is not a message or a demon-stration. It is just a life. Your life. Lived for reasons that do not require articulation.

∗ ∗ ∗

What This Book Was Really About

Let me tell you what this book was really about.

It was not about money. Money appeared in these pages because money is unavoidable, because the mechanics of free-dom require understanding the mechanics of financial security. But money was never the point. Money was the tool. The point was something else.

It was about removing friction. The friction between who you are and how you spend your days. The friction between what you value and what you do. The friction that accumu-lates when you live according to scripts you did not write, for reasons you never examined, toward destinations you never chose.

It was about making time visible. Time passes whether you attend to it or not. Most people do not attend. They sleepwalk through decades, assuming the future will arrive eventually, assuming they will get around to living eventually. This book was an attempt to wake you up, not with alarm, but with attention.

It was about reducing fear. Fear is what keeps people trapped. Fear of running out. Fear of judgment. Fear of the unknown that waits beyond the familiar misery of obligation. The formulas and frameworks in this book were not really about optimization. They were about demonstrating that the fear is smaller than it appears. That the path forward is walkable. That the monsters guarding the exit are mostly imaginary.

Money as tool, not outcome. Time as gift, not threat. Fear as signal, not master. This is what the book was for. Not to make you wealthy, but to make you aligned. To close the gap between the life you are living and the life you actually want.

The day I stopped worrying about wealth is the day I started generating it.

* * *

The Index Card

Here is the formula again. The whole thing. Simple enough to fit on an index card.

Open a brokerage account. It does not matter which one. Fidelity, Schwab, Vanguard. Pick any of them. They all work. The choice of brokerage is not where people fail. People fail by not opening the account at all.

Buy an index fund. A broad one. The S&P 500. A total market fund. Something that owns a piece of everything. Do not try to pick stocks. Do not try to time the market. Do not try to be clever. Clever loses to boring over decades, almost every time.

Automate contributions. Set it and forget it. One hundred dollars a month. Five hundred if you can. Whatever you can sustain without thinking about it. The amount matters less than the consistency. The consistency matters less than the time.

Then wait. That is the entire strategy. Open the account. Buy the fund. Automate. Wait.

Trust the system. Not because systems are always trustworthy, but because this particular system, diversified ownership of productive businesses across the economy, has a longer track record than any alternative. It has survived world wars, depressions, pandemics, and every prediction of imminent collapse. When you own an index fund, you own a piece of human enterprise. You are betting that people will continue to build things, solve problems, create value. That bet has paid off for over a century. It is the safest bet available.

This time is never different. Open the account. Trust the system. Wait.

*　*　*

Do This Now

Now let me speak directly to the parents.

Do this now.

Not when you have more money. Not when the timing is better. Not when you understand it all perfectly. Now.

Open an account for your child the week they are born. Fund it with whatever you can. Twenty dollars, fifty dollars, one hundred dollars. Set up automatic contributions. Then forget it exists.

By the time that child is eighteen, the account will contain something meaningful. Not because you contributed so much, but because time did the work. The gift is not the money. The gift is the lesson. The gift is showing them that the system works, that patience pays, that the future can be built deliberately rather than stumbled into.

You cannot control what your children will do with the money. You cannot guarantee they will be responsible. They might blow it on something stupid. They might make choices you would never make.

Let it go.

You cannot control another human being. Not your child, not anyone. The belief that you can, or should, is the source of enormous suffering. Your job is not to control the outcome. Your job is to provide the opportunity.

Teach them about compounding. Show them how the account grew while they were not watching. Explain the math, the patience, the power of time. Give them the information they need to make good decisions.

Then release. Whatever they do with it is their choice. Their life. Their lesson to learn.

The parents who wait for certainty never act. The parents who act despite uncertainty give their children something most people never receive: a head start, and an example.

Do it now. The timing will never be perfect. The amount will never be enough. Do it anyway.

* * *

Not Arriving Late

This book was not about retiring early. That framing, while useful, misses the deeper point.

This book was about not arriving late.

Late to your own life. Late to your second life. Late to the experiences that matter. Late to the people you love and the days you have been given. Late to the recognition that time is passing, that the years are accumulating, that the future you are deferring toward will arrive whether you are ready or not. Being able to enjoy every dime you worked hard to earn, save, or invest.

Most people arrive late. They spend decades in preparation, in accumulation, in the belief that life will begin after some condition is met. They wait for financial security, for the right moment, for permission. And then the moment comes, if it comes, and they discover that much of what they were waiting for is no longer available. The body has changed. The energy has changed. The people they meant to spend time with have moved on—or passed on. They arrive at freedom and find that freedom is smaller than it once would have been.

You do not have to arrive late.

Our life is the accumulation of stories so wait for nothing. Die with zero.

* * *

The Dividend

The reward for all of this work is not retirement. It is not even your second life.

It is presence.

The ability to notice. To actually see the people in front of you, rather than looking through them toward the next task. To hear what someone is saying, rather than rehearsing your response while they speak. To feel the texture of an ordinary moment, the warmth of the cup, the quality of the light, the particular way the air smells on this particular morning.

Presence is not a skill you acquire. It is what remains when you remove the obstacles. The urgency, the fear, the constant calculation, these are the obstacles. They fill your attention so completely that there is no room left for the moment you are actually in.

When the obstacles lift, presence returns. Not as achievement, but as default. You find yourself noticing things you had stopped seeing. The laugh lines around a friend's eyes. The way your child's voice has changed. The particular blue of the sky on a Tuesday afternoon. These were always there. You were just too busy to see them.

Joy follows presence. Not the loud joy of celebration, but the quiet joy of contact. The small pleasure of being fully in a conversation, fully in a meal, fully in a walk. You laugh more easily because you are actually there to catch the humor. You feel more deeply because you are not defended against your own experience.

This is the dividend. Not the money, though the money helped. Not the freedom, though the freedom created space. The dividend is presence itself. The experience of being alive while you are alive.

* * *

You Are Already Enough

I spent most of my life trying to be enough. To have enough. Only at fifty-four did I realize that no one really cared. Sure, they might enjoy watching me flame out, as humans, we do seem to like disasters. I finally realized that my enough is my enough. Once the foundation is set, you can choose to do or be anything you want, every single day.

You do not need to become anything else.

The digits in the account, the titles on the card, the labels on the possessions, none of them make you more yourself. They are decorations on a house that is already complete. You can add to the house. You can improve it. But the house was never insufficient. You were always living in it.

You can retire with one hundred, five hundred, or a million dollars. The number was never the point. The number was just how I kept score while I was learning what actually mattered.

This book is what I wish I had written first. Start here. The digits will follow, or they won't, and either way you'll be more prepared than I was.

* * *

My Parents' Son

I am my parents' son.

My mother talks to everyone. So do I. The cashier, the stranger in line, the person who clearly wants to be left alone. I can't help it. It's genetic. My father found his way to a fifty-five-and-over trailer park in Florida, working part-time at a nudist resort. He's at peace in a way I never saw when he was following the script. The lunch at the resort is great and the poolside band is awesome. We both needed to throw out the map before we could find somewhere that felt like home.

I am just like my parents. I spend too freely, trust too easily, talk too much, and believe that generosity is more important than accumulation. I inherited their patterns, their flaws, their stubborn insistence that life should feel like something.

I am just like them. One generation smarter. Smart enough to read the books they never read, ask the questions they never asked. Lucky enough to meet wealthy people who taught me new skills. That's it. That's the whole difference. Same raw material, different timing.

My parents accidentally gave me the dream. I just gave it a deadline.

That license plate still sits in my office. 55 AND OUT. I kept the promise for them. Not the way they imagined, not on their timeline, but close enough.

*　*　*

There is no next step. There is no action item. There is no final framework to implement or strategy to execute. There is just this moment, and then the next one, and then the next. Moments you can inhabit fully or moments you can rush through on your way to somewhere else. Make the deposit now, in your kids, in your relationships, in your future self.

Wealth is having the time to do whatever you want. Gaining wealth means patience.

Nothing is missing.

*　*　*

Questions Worth Sitting With

1. Who is your best friend? When did you last tell them? Who is your second best friend? Would they be surprised to hear it?

2. Who do you currently need permission from before you can make a big decision, a trip, a purchase, a change? Is that permission real, or is it a habit you never examined?

3. Imagine your life with unlimited time to do anything. What is the first thing you would do? Not the grandest thing. The first thing. That answer is closer to your truth than any five-year plan.

4. What would "nothing is missing" feel like in your life? Not perfection. Not completion. Just the quiet sense that you have enough, you are enough, and the day in front of you is yours.

5. If your children or grandchildren read this book thirty years from now, what is the one sentence you would want them to remember about how you lived?

About the Author

CHRISTOPHER JUSTICE is a technologist, executive, and lifelong builder whose career has spanned roles as CMO, CIO, and CEO across startups and enterprise environments.

An American with a global life, he has lived and worked in Austin, Florida, Switzerland, Armenia, and Portugal, and regularly takes unstructured sojourns to recalibrate—sometimes on a motorcycle across Europe, sometimes in a minivan with no agenda, occasionally while wearing a kilt.

His work blends systems thinking with lived reflection, shaped by decades of leadership, reinvention, and a growing appreciation for simplicity. He is interested less in accumulation than alignment, and less in optimization than presence. *55 and Out* is his most personal work to date.